MW01253367

MASCULINITY AND FEMININITY TODAY

Psychoanalysis & Women Series

MASCULINITY AND FEMININITY TODAY

Edited by

*Ester Palerm Marí and
Frances Thomson-Salo*

A Volume in the Psychoanalysis & Women Series
for the Committee on Women and Psychoanalysis
of the International Psychoanalytical Association

KARNAC

First published in 2013 by
Karnac Books Ltd
118 Finchley Road
London NW3 5HT

British Library Cataloguing in Publication Data

A C.I.P. for this book is available from the British Library

ISBN-13: 978-1-78049-190-5

Typeset by V Publishing Solutions Pvt Ltd., Chennai, India

Printed in Great Britain

www.karnacbooks.com

CONTENTS

v

ABOUT THE EDITORS AND CONTRIBUTORS

Jacqueline Amati Mehler is a training and supervising analyst of the Italian Psychoanalytical Association and has made an important contribution to psychoanalysis in the realm of language and symbolisation. Dr. Amati Mehler has explored the "psycho-archaeology" of language, embedded in early affect and psychosensory experiences related to primary object relationships and primary processes. She has published a number of books in Italian and English.

Giovanna Ambrosio is a full member of the Italian Psychoanalytical Association and of the IPA, past secretary of the Italian Psychoanalytical Association, and chief editor of the journal *Psicoanalisi*. She is the immediate past chair of the IPA Committee on Women and Psychoanalysis (COWAP) and former European co-chair of the Committee on Women and Psychoanalysis (2001–2005). She edited "Transvestism, Transsexualism in the Psychoanalytic Dimension" in the Controversies in Psychoanalysis series.

Rui Aragão Oliveira, PhD in clinical psychology, is member of the Portuguese Psychoanalytical Society (component society of the International Psychoanalytical Association). He is a research member of the Psychology and Health Research Unit, ISPA/Lisbon. He works in private practice in Lisbon.

Martina Burdet Dombald is a full member of the Psychoanalytic Association of Madrid (APM), and currently is a member of the board of directors of the APM. She has published various papers on the subject of gender violence and masochism in women, and has explored issues of general interest to men and women.

Michael J. Diamond, PhD, FIPA, is a practicing clinical psychologist and psychoanalyst and the author of the book *My Father Before Me: How Fathers & Sons Influence Each Other Throughout Their Lives*. Dr. Diamond is currently a training and supervising analyst at the Los Angeles Institute and Society for Psychoanalytic Studies, an associate clinical professor of psychiatry at UCLA and is on the faculty at the Wright Institute Los Angeles. Dr. Diamond has written numerous articles and publications on fathering and father-son relationships.

Emilce Dio Bleichmar, MD, PhD, is a member of the Argentine Psychoanalytic Association, director and professor of the postgraduate course: "Clinic and Psychoanalytic Psychotherapy of the Child and His/Her Family", director of the department of Women´s Studies ELIPSIS, a teaching institution of the Pontificia Comillas University, Madrid; vice-president of Forum Psychoanalytic Psychotherapy Society, editorial reader of the International Forum of Psychoanalysis (Sweden) journal, and a member of the International Attachment Network (IAN). She has published widely.

Antònia Grimalt, MD, is a psychoanalyst working with children, adolescents, and adults in Barcelona. She is a training analyst and director of the Training Institute of the Spanish Psychoanalytical Society and member of the forum for child psychoanalysis in the European Psychoanalytic Federation.

Irene Oromí is a member of the Spanish Psychoanalytical Society and presented "Educational therapy as a possible way to repair a deficit in the primary relationship" at the 7th International Educational Therapy Conference, Norway.

Ester Palerm Marí, MD and clinical psychologist, is a member of the Spanish Psychoanalytical Society (SEP), a component society of the

International Psychoanalytic Association. Dr. Palerm served on the Board of Directors of the SEP from 2008 to 2012. She was part of the staff of the Psychosomatic Unit at the Hospital de St. Pau i la Santa Creu in Barcelona both in the capacity of physician and psychologist for several years, and now has a private practice in Barcelona where she works as a psychoanalyst and psychotherapist for children, adolescents and adults. She has written papers on a diverse number of themes such as pregnancy, delivery and the postpartum period, the psycho-bio-social framework of assisting chronic patients, the elderly, and the terminally ill, sexuality, and counter transference. Her COWAP-related activities include coordinating and participating in workshops at European COWAP conferences. Dr. Palerm was the coordinator of the COWAP meeting held in Barcelona in 2011 "Feminine and Masculine Today".

Teresa Rocha Leite Haudenschild is a training analyst and child and adolescent analyst of the Brazilian Psychoanalytical Society of São Paulo. She is a liaison member of COWAP for the Brazilian Psychoanalytical Federation. She has presented and published widely, including "Flashes of selected events in non-verbal levels of communication apprehension", "The green continent", "The father and the constitution of masculinity", and on the mother's gaze.

James S. Rose is a member of the British Psychoanalytical Society and editor of *Mapping Psychic Reality: Triangulation, Communication, and Insight*, a book about how we can deepen our understanding of subjectivity through the use of the concept of triangulation. He has presented internationally including on a COWAP panel at the 2011 EPF conference in Copenhagen.

Frances Thomson-Salo is an honorary principal fellow of the department of psychiatry, University of Melbourne, and a member of the British Psychoanalytic Society and immediate past president of the Australian Psychoanalytical Association. She is a member of the board of the International Journal of Psychoanalysis, and chair of the IPA Committee on Women in Psychoanalysis. She is an honorary fellow of the Murdoch Children's Research Institute, the consultant infant mental health clinician, Royal Women's Hospital, Melbourne, and is teaching faculty for the University of Melbourne Graduate Diploma/Masters in infant and parent mental health. She is the psychoanalyst-in-residence for The Dax Centre of artworks and has published in the fields of child psychoanalysis and infant mental health.

Majlis Winberg Salomonsson is a child and adult psychoanalyst in private practice in Stockholm, Sweden, and a training analyst and former director of the training institute in the Swedish Psychoanalytic Association. She also works as a teacher and supervisor. She has written books and articles on the subject of development and psychoanalytic treatment of children and adolescents. She is doing research at the department of women´s and children´s health at Karolinska Institutet, Stockholm.

ACKNOWLEDGEMENTS

We wish to thank, not only the authors who contributed so generously to this book, but also those who contributed to making the publication of this book possible, especially those who joined Ester Palerm Marí in Barcelona in making this become a reality. Many thanks, therefore, go to M. Areny, G. Callicó, C. García-Catrillón, A. Luengo, S. Lupinacci, I. Miró, P. Tardío, E. Torras de Beà, and also to the board of directors of the Spanish Psychoanalytical Society (2008–2012), and most especially President A. Pérez-Sánchez. We also wish to thank all of those who have in any way, however indirectly, sponsored this book. Lastly, and above all, we thank the International Psychoanalytical Association for their ongoing commitment to the work of the Committee on Women and Psychoanalysis.

We also thank W. W. Norton & Company for citation permission for the excerpt of the Stephen Dunn poem, "Achilles in love" (published by W. W. Norton & Company in 2004 in the collection entitled *The Insistence of Beauty*, on pp. 66–67), and to italicise it in Chapter One.

And we thank Quino (Joaquín Salvador Lavado) for permission to include the Mafalda strip in Chapter Nine.

INTRODUCTION

Ester Palerm Marí and Frances Thomson-Salo

Masculinity and femininity today

A wide range of authors have contributed to this book, sometimes integrating theoretical points in quite novel ways, sometimes making quite controversial points which are likely to stir lively debate; in doing so, the authors have enabled us to reflect further on issues of masculinity and femininity today.

This book addresses what is currently understood by "masculinity" and "femininity" in psychoanalytic terms. As Glocer Fiorini (2007) reminds us: "In the field of psychoanalysis, there is no single perspective on sexual difference or on the concepts of masculinity and femininity" (p. 122); and "The tendency to consider femininity as a problematic topic derives from the theories concerning the sexual difference" (p. 130). The book addresses two perspectives: the first is to what extent the characteristics of both are present in each individual, and how they can be recognised in patients of both sexes. From the second perspective the authors, taking into account "masculinity" and "femininity" as present in the analyst, whether they are male or female, consider how this reflects in their analytic work and what limitations this may imply in the development of the "feminine" analytic function in a male analyst, and vice versa.

Michael Diamond, in "Evolving perspectives on masculinity and its discontents: Reworking the internal phallic and genital positions", gives an overview of psychoanalytic understanding of masculinity and male development, clarifying what he means by phallic and genital masculinity, and focuses on the internalisation processes impacting masculine gender identity. He then reflects on the interplay between the male's initial sense of masculinity, his uniquely gendered ego ideal, and the central developmental challenges in reworking the phallic and genital positions, making reference to developing an interiorised dimension of genital masculinity to do with the inner body that reflects the more open and receptive aspects of male psychic experience. He questions the Freudian hypothesis that the male child must disidentify with the mother, and identify with the father in order to separate from the mother. The boy´s separation from his mother is achieved with the aid of his father; through the father-son relationship the child is helped to separate from his mother, not in opposition to femininity, but rather through the love he has for his father, assisted by the ability his father has to facilitate the new bond with him, containing the anxiety inherent in this process. In other words, a process of differentiation and progressive separation takes place that permits the boy´s masculinity to be founded on a reciprocal identification with an available father and with a mother who is capable of admitting and affirming her son´s masculinity. That is to say, a couple capable of recognising and loving their son.

In the young adult these traits are associated with assertiveness, strength, potency, the achievement of wishes and ambitions, and competitive cravings. All of these are fundamental for the accomplishment of one´s ambitions. In a more developed process, this is complemented by the masculine capacity to confer the same importance to the partner´s satisfaction as to one´s own satisfaction, and the faculty of achieving a bond and intimacy with others becomes more significant. When defensive aspects predominate, a character disorder may be present to protect the frail and inflexible masculine identity that defines itself by a self-demonstration of exhibitionism and arrogance; the masculine attributes are then considered more of an instrument of aggression than of love, and imply recklessness, misogyny, and an excessive need to demonstrate one´s own abilities. In other words, a man´s rejection of his "feminine" self indicates a failure at optimal development, and a denial of his capacity to be nurturing and to procreate.

Giovanna Ambrosio, while still finding some common ground with aspects of Diamond's conceptualisation, critiques aspects of this paper quite vigorously from a different theoretical approach. She puts forward that a mature genital organisation requires the complete recognition of oneself and of the other in his/her totality. This is an ideal for men as much as it is for women. She points out the importance of differentiating between the most primitive levels that precede the organisation of individuation and, therefore, from the identification of later degrees of identity. She also points out the clinical importance of differentiating between the more primitive degrees of identity, where the child imitates mother or father, and the more mature feeling of identity, which is the product of the never-ending process of introjection, organisation, and integration that arises from the bond and the interaction with the father and the mother.

James Rose, in his contribution, "The hour of the stranger" focuses in a more clinical paper on how adolescents discover their sexuality and come to "own" their sexual bodies as they grow towards adulthood. He speaks to the impact made on the adolescent by a body that is not recognised, and the flowering of sensations where the body, mind, sexuality, and identity undergo changes and acquire new dimensions. In addition to two clinical vignettes—of an adolescent girl and an adolescent boy respectively—he draws widely on references to English and to French literature, and, by way of illustration, specifically to the protagonists of the novel by Colette, *Le Blé en Herbe*. The writer describes two children in this novel—a boy and a girl—who, having grown up together, and shared in the same play, suddenly erupt into adolescence, which separates them and changes everything between them for evermore. They become aware that not only has their concept of their own bodies changed, but also their idea of the body of the opposite sex. The idea of the complementarity of the sexes appears here. The two sexes must take into their awareness of themselves the fact of their sexual bodies, and also the possibility of a new relationship with a member of the opposite sex.

The commencement of adolescence, as announced by the appearance of puberty, represents a disruption in development because the individual experiences the possibility and likelihood of something new and radically different in life. When adolescents, therefore, ask an adult for help, it means that they are willing to face the consequences of an encounter with the stranger within themselves and within the other. This willingness is not conscious, but must be expressed in the anxiety that their call for help awakens. They will frequently say that it is difficult for them to talk about themselves. Their desire to remain in silence reflects the desire to keep a sense of self, and also their fear that their sense of self will be subverted if they open up to the other person. We are dealing with a self which is being shaped, and that protects itself from intrusion, and not necessarily from fear of intimacy, as could be the case with an adult. We could say that adolescents are in the process of "getting to know themselves", and that they do not want this process compromised by an adult who believes he or she will be able to understand them before they can understand themselves.

Antònia Grimalt, in a discussion of this, further explores what is understood by masculinity and femininity in current psychoanalytic terms, highlighting the adolescent discovery of sexuality and the process of mentalisation of his/her body, and particularly the concrete presence of an absence. Grimalt also considers how "masculine" and "feminine" reflect in analytic work and the limitations this may imply in the development of the "feminine" analytic function or the "masculine" analytic function, depending on whether the analyst is a woman or a man. She points out the importance of primary relationships, and the consequences of problems in these early bonds. The child who has not experienced the necessary mental security to differentiate from the primary object will remain submerged in a world dominated by the emotional processes of the other. She nuances the need to differentiate, in adolescence, between the *no communication* put to the service of having one´s own experience and preserving a sense of self in a creative process of differentiation, from an activity of adolescent withdrawal and fantasising closer to sensorium and in the service of recreating a lost fusion. Emotional disorder is the consequence of the dissociation between the feminine and masculine elements of the personality—one part that cannot contain the other, and vice versa. If this dissociation is not resolved then the sensorial relationship with no affective implication is sought out, or the search for a relationship altogether is inhibited.

Jacqueline Amati Mehler explores, in her chapter "The abyss of intimacy", some of the problems encountered in male sexuality, and in particular as they manifest in male impotence. She expounds on the importance that sensuality (associated with the pleasure that the sense organs provide) and affects be integrated into human relationships. A failure in this integration results in splitting and, in consequence, sensual aspects and affects, and sexual desire, will seek gratification in different objects.

Martina Burdet Dombald expands on "Lack of discrimination as a defence mechanism", making use of a recent novel that enjoyed wide popularity, and the example of a very successful pop star, both of which exhibit confused and undifferentiated masculine and feminine traits. She analyses situations where it appears that no clear discrimination between masculinity and femininity exists, that is, situations in which there is a denial of sexual differences. This cult of undifferentiated-ness can, in neurotic patients, represent the manner in which the mental apparatus protects itself when facing anxieties of exclusion and differentiation, or, conversely, reflect the greatest of all anxieties—that of fragmentation or, in borderline pathology, of not existing.

Teresa Haudenschild in "Listening to psychical bisexuality in analysis" discusses the analyst having a sufficiently elaborated psycho-bisexuality, that is, "a good internalised parental couple", which presupposes the differentiation of gender and generations. By means of the analyst's own internal reference, the internal "faults" of the patients may be discerned: insufficient internalisation of a maternal or paternal figure—insufficiencies often due to transgenerational factors—to "faults" in the make-up in the mental structure of the parents of these patients.

Rui Aragão Oliveira considers, in "Masculinity and the analytic relationship", in particular the transforming of masculinity in the course of the analysis, from identification with the mother to identification with a father figure. He points out that development of a masculine identity is facilitated by the good quality of early relationships between the boy and his mother, and not by the quality of his separation from the mother. The establishment of masculinity begins with the appearance of the third person—the father. This appearance initially begins as contact with the "father in the mind of the mother". This can start even before the mother realises it, when she presents herself as "the mother-wife-of-the-father".

Emilce Dio Bleichmar, in her paper "Intersubjective context of gender and sexuality", defends the concept of gender as a broad and complex self structure, shaped from the beginning by the unconscious intersubjective interchange between the parental figures and their sons and daughters. She says that for this reason it is advisable to broaden the way in which the analyst listens to patients, and to tune in better to the manner in which women speak about restrictions to self and the difficulties which they encounter when they make the decision to differentiate themselves from the feminine model that their mothers represent. She indicates the importance of listening to and separating this anxiety from oedipal conflicts.

Lastly, there are two chapters on child psychoanalysis. In the first, in a paper, "Identity: A constellation of emotional experience and metaphors in childhood", Irene Oromí presents her young child patient's struggle with issues regarding developmentally appropriate but potentially pathological sexuality, all of which she conveys in a very vivid and moving way. She begins with the symptomatology of a boy with difficulties in concentrating and learning, who played only with girls, being hit and debased by other boys, and traces his early development in order to understand his difficulties in building up an awareness of self and a gender identity. She shows how, during his development, the process of his sense of identity was affected when his bodily sensations were not linked to the emotion that the presence of his parents caused in him. This failure brought about an enclave in the boy's mental organisation, thus predisposing to development of a false identity. As a child analyst, she considers that the question is not what masculinity or femininity is, but rather to understand the case individually with each patient's motivations and suffering.

In the second chapter, in a paper entitled "Furious with love: Some reflections on the sexuality of a little girl", Majlis Winberg Salomonsson presents three sessions of analysis to show us how infantile sexuality appears at this stage of development, drawing for her understanding on some illustrations taken from childhood stories. In the first session she shows how, through play, the child exhibits phallic aspects, and how these influence her masculine and feminine identifications, as well as the presence of the primary scene in play. At the same time she raises the issue of how to capture these identifications in the analytic relationship. The second session takes place while the child sleeps. This does not prevent the analyst, who makes use of her child patient's associations to the story of Sleeping Beauty, from practicing her analytic function, questioning the presence and meaning of her sleep at that moment. The third session is once again active and, again through play, the patient´s changing identifications, reflecting the underlying anxieties, are made overt.

Reference

Glocer Fiorini, L. (2007). *Deconstructing the Feminine: Psychoanalysis, Gender and Theories of Complexity*. London: Karnac.

CHAPTER ONE

Evolving perspectives on masculinity and its discontents: reworking the internal phallic and genital positions

Michael J. Diamond

This chapter presents an overview of my psychoanalytic understanding of masculinity and male development. I clarify what I mean by phallic and genital masculinity, and briefly address the roles played by both biology and culture in influencing how boys establish their earliest sense of masculinity. I then focus on the internalisation processes impacting masculine gender identity prior to reflecting upon the interplay between the male's initial sense of masculinity, his uniquely gendered ego ideal, and the central developmental challenges that ensue in reworking the phallic and genital positions. To set us on course, I begin by offering a contemporary perspective on gender.

A contemporary perspective on gender

Where Freud did *not* use the terms gender or gender identity nor explore such areas, several generations of psychoanalytic theorists have grappled with gender related issues as well as gender questions raised by Freud's (1925) original ideas on psychosexual development. As you recall, Freud (1925) tackled these issues originally through his account of how the young child's discovery of the anatomical differences between the sexes, with the resulting castration anxiety or penis envy, influences male and female development, conflicts, and personality. As Kulish (2010) suggested, contemporary thinking about gender can be organised into five major, interrelated areas: (1) the social construction of gender; (2) the complexity and fluidity of gender; (3) the separation of gender and object choice; (4) normality versus marginality; and (5) embodiment. I primarily consider the first two areas.

Though probably obvious, the landscape of psychoanalysis and gender abounds with conceptual, terminological, technical, and socio-political difficulties. Not surprisingly, gender, with its basis in differentiation and an accompanying history of gender-based suffering and oppression, is a minefield where disturbance is to be expected (see Benjamin, 1996; Harris, 1991). Yet today, much as when Freud started his psychosexual prospecting, there continues to be something about the terrain that draws us close to the heart of the mind-body-spirit interface. And happily, we now have an assortment of canvassing tools that Freud did not.

Nowadays we are more likely to understand that gender identity development is *not* a linear, continuous trajectory, and that a boy's (and later, a man's) experience of the ambiguities of his gender are continually being reworked across differing developmental junctions (see Diamond, 1997, 1998, 2004a, 2004b, 2006, 2007, 2009). Moreover, in bridging the polarities between social *constructionism* and biological *essentialism*, a more complicated, and ambiguous, understanding of gender identity ensues that is constructed largely out of early, preoedipal identifications with each parent (in addition to being influenced by biological variables). A healthy sense of masculinity requires incorporating the multitude of these early identifications (as well as subsequent ones) and inevitably demands a psychic achievement in the integrative-synthetic sphere. Hence, the analyst's clinical understanding of male patients' unconscious conflicts around gender-related issues, as well as personal gender-related biases and countertransferences, can lead to more effective interpretive interventions.

Masculinity and psychoanalysis

Until three or four decades ago, the psychoanalytic study of male development was essentially organised around Freud's oedipal theory and the idea that the boy wants to *have* his mother (Freud, 1923, 1924, 1925).

To overcome the castration anxieties aroused in competing with his father, the boy identifies with him and, in turn, constructs the sense of his own masculine identity. Moreover, by equating masculinity with activity and femininity with passivity, as Freud (1937) exemplified in referring to the male's bedrock struggle "against his passive or feminine attitude toward another male" (p. 250), he furthered "the rejection of femininity" (De Simone Gaburri, 1985, p. 466). Indeed, Freud (ibid., pp. 252–253) argues that the repudiation of femininity, the so-called "masculine protest" (which is "nothing else than castration anxiety"), reflects a "biological fact". This confusion between both receptivity and passivity, and between psychodynamics and biology, continues to collude with cultural assumptions and hinders psychoanalytic theorising about masculinity.

Nonetheless, by the latter third of the twentieth century, attention had been redirected to the fact that before the boy wants to *have* his mother, he wants to *be* his mother, or at least *be with* what his mother provides, that is, her maternal nurturance. Hence, the boy's *preoedipal* relationship with his mother, and the actual involvement of the father in the early triadic environment, is now seen as crucial to understanding male gender identity.

Analysts influenced by Margaret Mahler (cf. Mahler, Pine, & Bergman, 1975) began to formulate a new way of understanding male psychology. Most significant were Ralph Greenson and Robert Stoller, who formulated what has become known as the *disidentification hypothesis* (Greenson, 1966, 1968; Stoller, 1964, 1965, 1968, 1976), claiming that in order to establish a normal, healthy sense of masculinity, the small boy must *dis*-identify *from* his mother and *counter*-identify *with* his father. This idea has been taken as the benchmark to explain the male's struggle to experience his gendered identity as "masculine".

The theory happens to be congruent with a dubious, widely held view in patriarchal cultures that masculinity is defined by its *not* being feminine. In other words, the most significant thing about being a man is *not being a woman*. This reductive and monolithic view has been unfortunate for both sexes but perhaps especially so for men, since gender identity, as long as it is based on the disavowal of whatever is construed as feminine (and that persists in being equated with passivity), remains an unstable psychological achievement.

More recent work by psychoanalytic gender theorists, however, has furthered our understanding of boys' earliest and subsequent sense of masculinity (e.g., Axelrod, 1997; Benjamin, 1988, 1991; Fast, 1984, 1990, 1999; Hansell, 1998; Lax, 1997; Pollack, 1995, 1998;). Furthermore, Freud's famous dictum that "anatomy is destiny" is no longer the lynchpin of psychoanalytic gender theorising. Research on the masculinisation of the brain demonstrates that several biological variables are related to male specific gender-related traits, challenges, and intrapsychic conflicts (Baron-Cohen, 2003; Panksepp, 1998). Nonetheless, on the basis of clinical evidence, the biological givens in gender identity formation are significantly counterbalanced by what psychoanalysis emphasises: the early imprinting of the boy's actual interactions with his primary attachment figures; his internalised object relations; the prevailing socio-cultural determinants; and most important, his unique psychodynamically determined reactions to each of these influences, particularly as they interact with his basic biological development (cf. Blos, 1984; Stoller, 1976). We might say therefore that with respect to biology, *the destiny of a boy's masculinity is based on what he makes of his anatomy*!

Contemporary psychoanalytic theory must be able to sustain the necessary dialectical tension between biological givens, such as hormonally influenced brain and bodily masculinisation, and the psychosocially created—that is, between traditional essentialist (either-or thinking) and a postmodern, constructivist (both-and) perspective. Thus, it is important to maintain the dialectical tension between the dichotomous (or fixed) aspects of gender experience and the more integrated experience of gender, between gender *rigidity* and *fluidity,* and between (*core*) *gender identity* and the *gender multiplicity of the multigendered self.*

However, as cultural beings we cannot so easily contain this tension. Anthropologists write about a ubiquitous socio-cultural process that renders a splitting of gender traits so that aspects of human personality are distributed unequally between the sexes (see Young-Eisendrath, 1997; also Labouvie-Vief, 1994). In every culture, gender polarity is internalised, and each child is directed to develop qualities attributed to their own sex and, in some measure, to suppress or disavow qualities of the other—to keep the other gender's characteristics less developed within (see Young-Eisendrath, 1997). This occurs even though hormonal influences on the foetal brain and genitalia demonstrate differences between the two genders. Regardless of how we define the concepts of masculine and feminine from a constitutional perspective, what is most serviceable in psychoanalysis stems from clinical observation that demonstrates that "… in human beings pure masculinity or femininity is *not* to be found in either a psychological or a biological sense. Every individual on the contrary displays a mixture of the character-traits belonging to his own and to the opposite sex; and he shows a combination of activity and passivity whether or not these last character-traits tally with his biological ones" (Freud, 1905, p. 220n).

Culture indeed plays a pivotal role in interfacing with the psychodynamics of gender identity—there are a wide variety of masculinities across cultures—and masculinity is *not* the exclusive province of heterosexual men (cf. Person, 2006). In Western societies, despite efforts to reduce this gender splitting, the underlying cultural images for masculinity generally continue to mean being rational, protective, aggressive, and dominating, while those for femininity mean being emotional, nurturing, receptive, and submissive (Benjamin, 1988).

Fogel (2006), in underscoring our inherent *psychological* bisexuality, suggests, like our Jungian colleagues, that dialectical balance between the *masculine principle*, characterised by boundaries, definitions, penetration, differentiation, and doing, and the contrasting *feminine*, represented by fluidity, receptivity, creativity, containment, integration, space, and being, is required for healthy maturation. Thus, psychoanalysis must comprehend the implications of the "lost feminine half", recognizing the "dark hole" in a man's inner genital position (Fogel, 2006, p. 1143–1144; see also Elise, 2001 in her discussion of "phallic supremacy").

An evolving perspective on masculinity

In my own work, I revise the disidentification model, emphasise how masculinity is forged from the boy's earliest wishes to be *both* his mother and father, and suggest how the male's earliest identifications require adaptations and accommodations throughout the life span (Diamond, 1998, 2004a, 2004b, 2006, 2009). Likewise, a male's gendered ego ideals and his sense of masculinity, as well as the ambiguities of his gender, are continually being reworked throughout his life. The *phallic* and *genital features* of a man's internal experience are best understood as coexisting positions in varying, discontinuous balances that shift as a man matures (much like the Kleinian notion of paranoid-schizoid and depressive positions), rather than representing different developmental phases that supersede one another linearly.

Terminology: phallic and genital masculinity

A brief word on terminology is needed. In using the terms *phallic* and *genital*, I am referring to a specific orientation, typically manifest in a cluster of traits, which psychoanalysis views as originating from early psychosexual, libidinal development. From the classical standpoint, the *phallic phase* refers to that pre-genital period beginning at about two years of age and extending into the oedipal phase, during which the phallus is the primary erogenous zone. Freud (1923) describes this "infantile" organisation as reflecting "a primacy of the *phallus*" rather than of the genitals (original italics, p. 142). The phase comprises two subphases: *phallic narcissism* (or, *phallic exhibitionism*), characterised by a self-satisfaction based on an overestimation of the penis, exhibitionistic desires to gain attention, and the primacy of dyadic relations, and the later *phallic-oedipal phase proper* with its triangular configuration, idealisation of oedipal objects promoting phallic omnipotence, and heightened castration anxieties (see Edgcumbe & Burgner, 1975; Greenspan, 1982; Jones, 1933; Schalin, 1989).

Throughout the entire phallic phase, the high valuation of the penis is manifest in phallic pride with its associated desires and anxieties. Figuratively speaking, extending, thrusting, and penetrating become paramount along with the associated personality traits of assertiveness, aggression, strength, and potency in the realisation of one's desire.

Such phallic ambitions, propensities, and energies are utilised, integrated, and transformed throughout a male's development and these phallic features of internal life will play an important role in males *adaptively* expressing and experiencing their masculinity. These healthy phallic aspects are evident in the male's embracing of his desires and ambitions, pursuits, competitive yearnings, delights in bodily pleasures, and hierarchical relations as well as his capacities for achievement, penetration, and dominance.

In contrast, the male's *defensive phallicity* frequently reflects more transitory regressive tendencies in an otherwise healthy personality; alternatively, it may indicate more rigid characterological distortions based upon primitive defensive operations employed to protect his fragile, inflexible masculine gender identity. In the latter case, the so-called "phallic character" is characterised by exhibitionistic self-display, haughty reserve, a regarding of the penis as an instrument of aggression (rather than love), recklessness, misogyny, and an excessive need to display one's potency. Such pathology can manifest at varying developmental junctures, though is traditionally understood as regressively based on oedipal-phase anxieties (see Jones, 1933). This is evident in adult men who persist in defining themselves by conquest, sexual potency, and aggression when relational needs, a greater appreciation of otherness, and reflectivity might otherwise come to the fore.

The *genital phase* is considered the final stage in instinctual libidinal development, representing what Freud (1905) called "genital primacy". This primacy or "genital love" is traditionally understood as combining genital *satisfaction* with pregenital *tenderness* (Balint, 1948). The term "genital" more broadly reflects the male's capacity to attach equal importance to his own and his partner's satisfaction. Thus, the male's relational needs and abilities to achieve connection to, and intimacy with, others become more significant. This requires the man to develop and utilise an interiorised, culturally minimised dimension of genital masculinity pertaining to the inner body and testicles, the *inner genital space*, that reflects the more open, spatial, and receptive aspects of male psychic experience (e.g., Fogel, 1998; Friedman, 1996; Kestenberg, 1968), perhaps akin to what Bion (1965, 1970) considered the *void* (and "formless infinite").

In this realm, there is an expansion of bodily-sensual pleasure beyond the satisfactions associated with the penis so that the genital male enjoys both a wider range of visceral excitation (Bordo, 1999; Reis, 2009) and his own seminal procreative space (Figlio, 2010). In other words, both heterosexual *and* homosexual men yearn not only for the pleasures of the penis-in-vagina and/or penis-in-anus, but also to enjoy being penetrated, having one's testicles or breasts stimulated, experiencing seminal ejaculation involving both retention and release, feeling pleasure through the use of their mouths, and fantasising as well as engaging in a variety of sexual practices that are too easily societally pathologised (Figlio, 2010; Reis, 2009; see also Ferenczi, 1924). In short, maturing, healthy genitality is characterised by the attenuation of the anxieties pertaining both to masculine inner space and to non-penis dominated sensuality, as well as the lessening of anxieties associated with their psychical sensibilities. Penetration and receptivity, as well as intrusion and inclusion, are its hallmarks, whereas aims for connection and the recognition of the subjectivity of others (i.e., "otherness") indicate this postambivalent integration of phallic propensities.

The term *genitality*, as I use it, involves adaptive assertion, aggression, and modulated phallicism, in which penetration in the service of mastery, potency, and authority is *integrated with* the needs for creativity, connection, and attachment. Phallic urges are present and remain significant, but in their genital countenance they are transformed into more aim-inhibited and object-recognising forms. Both the *hierarchical* and the *relational* facets of maleness become part of a man's complex yet more flexible psychic structure. In this respect, there is a strong resemblance between the analytic ideal of the genital character and both the Anglo-Saxon prototype of a gentleman and the Judeo-Hebraic exemplar of a *mensch*. The maturing man's genital features help him to become oriented more towards making love rather than simply fucking—though of course the impulse to fuck remains an important dimension of his masculinity and lovemaking.

Thus, to paraphrase Freud, in order to truly understand "what men really want", we need to appreciate the challenges pertaining to reworking the internal phallic and genital positions across the course of a man's life. Next, I consider the initial challenge, which pertains to how male gender identity develops.

Male gender identity development

The internalisation processes involved during a boy's unique struggle to differentiate from his mother profoundly affect his forming a sense of himself as a male. The boy's separation from the world of his mother is a complex process that is evident for instance when, at around the age of three, he experiences a momentous alteration that, caused by his body's maturation, drives newly intense genital sensations. This arrival of sexuality is quite disruptive, partially because it also represents the loss of innocence in relationship to his mother. Bollas (2000) calls this "the death of infancy" (p. 15) wherein the "mother-as-comforter" becomes the "mother-as-sex-object".

Regarding the formation of male gender identity, my ideas depart from Greenson's (1968) prevailing "proto-feminine" normative model, in which infant boys develop in a feminine direction (Diamond, 2004a; 2004b; 2006). Whereas Freud originally understood gender as stemming from the fact that masculinity was the natural state for both sexes, Greenson and Stoller proposed that boys are naturally proto-feminine and must learn to renounce their femininity in order to achieve healthy gender identity. Today, there is no evidence to support such proto-femininity and most contemporary theorists view both masculinity and femininity *not* as innate but rather as having preoedipal origins in one's earliest relationships, identifications, and fantasies (Brady, 2006; Person, 2006).

In challenging this model wherein boys must *disidentify with* their mothers, *repudiate* their feminine identifications, and *counter-identify* with their fathers, I argue that such forceful splitting is both theoretically and clinically problematic, as well as ultimately indicative of substantial psychopathology (see also Axelrod, 1997; Fast, 1984, 1990, 1999).

The problem with disidentification

There is abundant evidence that little boys do tend to move away physically from their mothers and toward their fathers (or surrogates) to establish themselves as "boys" among males (Abelin, 1975; Gilmore, 1990; Mahler, Pine, & Bergman, 1975; Stoller, 1964, 1965; see also Freud, 1921). How do we understand this psychoanalytically? Is this "moving away" a prerequisite for a male's psychological development? (some cross-cultural data suggest otherwise). More to the point, is it necessary for a boy to create a mental barrier against his desire to maintain closeness with his mother?

To answer these questions, let us consider masculinity in the clinical sphere where we frequently encounter patients with conflicted, fragile, damaged masculine self-images. Traditionally, these internal conditions are understood as expressions of "too little" or "too much" masculinity. However, the clinical picture is far more muddied than prevailing notions of masculinity might suggest since we often see evidence of both too little masculinity in our male patients' inhibited aggression and overt passivity and too much masculinity in their phallic insistence on staving off emotional experience, including depending on the analyst and fearing being penetrated (as for example, by their analyst's eyes or words).

It is noteworthy that Greenson (1968; see also 1966), to support his preoedipal thesis for treating men, used a case example of Lance, a "transsexual-transvestite five-and-a-half-year-old boy" whose mother hated and "disrespected her husband and men in general", while his father "was absent … and had little if any pleasurable contact with the boy" (pp. 371–372). Employing clinical material reflective of a quite disturbed family system, Greenson generalised that Lance's "problems in disidentifying" were both developmentally normative and extremely meaningful in understanding "realistic gender identity" formation (p. 371).

What disidentification actually reflects

Pathological systems, in which Lance was enmeshed, are characteristic of families unable to triangulate successfully. Such pathological forms of early triangulation are set in motion by: (a) mothers who are severely misattuned to the individuation needs of their young sons or are misandryous; (b) fathers who are either weak and unavailable or misogynist; (c) a parental couple prone to splitting; and/or (d) the child's own biological constitution, temperament, and drive endowment, particularly with respect to what neuroscientists refer to as "brain and bodily masculinization" (Panksepp, 1998) and what psychoanalysts broadly term "merger proneness" (see also Abelin, 1971, 1975, 1980; Axelrod, 1997; Fast, 1984, 1990; Diamond, 1998, 2004b, 2006, 2009).

Under any or all of these circumstances, early gender identity development takes on the quality of a conflict or struggle, as Greenson suggests, and the little boy will tend to internalise the father's (and the mother's) contemptuous, devaluing attitude towards women. When this defensively based disidentification occurs, a pathological phallic rigidity commonly results. Thus, a zero sum game operates in which masculinity requires that femininity be relinquished. Engaging in denial and disavowal of maternal identifications, the young boy attempts to expel from consciousness early identifications typically grounded in more pathological triangular relations. What has been recently termed *femiphobia*—an unconscious hatred and dread of the part of the self that is experienced as feminine—often ensues (see Ducat, 2004). In other words, the male's repudiation of his "feminine" self signals a failure in optimum development and is evident in a defensively phallic organisation that denies a man's "procreative capacity and nurturing possibilities" (Fast, 1984, p. 73). I suspect that Freud (1937) had something like this in mind when he argued that a successful "terminable" analysis could only occur during those rare occasions when the male's bedrock struggle against his passive or feminine attitude is reached.

Revisioning boys turning away from their mothers

In contrast, under "good enough" conditions, the boy's turning away from his mother is *transitional* (Diamond, 1998; Fast, 1999). This transitional turning away from the mother helps the boy to differentiate and separate from his primary external object. However, this is *not* the same as "disidentifying" from his *internal* maternal object. In fact, the boy's particular experience of loss actually facilitates his internalisation of key aspects of his relationship with his mother. Identification occurs when there is a disruption to sufficiently gratifying emotional ties to a primary other (Loewald, 1962). Such internalisation builds psychic structure as "the child reaches out to take back … what has been removed from him" (Loewald, 1962, p. 496). Through this structuring process, renounced external objects, such as the mother whom the boy turns away from, become internal objects as the internal relationship becomes substituted for an external one. In fact, attachment research (Fonagy, 2001) suggests that a boy's secure sense of masculine identity develops from the quality of the boy-to-mother attachment (not separation), which is termed *attachment-individuation* rather than *separation-individuation* (see Lyons-Ruth, 1991).

Disidentification is actually a misnomer because early identifications are never simply removed nor repudiated in the unconscious once and for all (if they were, there would surely be less need for psychoanalysis). Rather, the boy's early identifications with his mother and father remain significant in his psychic structure; typically they become more accessible as he matures (see Diamond, 2004a).

In healthier forms of early gender identity development, progressive differentiation rather than opposition predominates, enabling masculinity to be founded upon a reciprocal identification with an available father (or surrogate), a mother who is able to recognise and affirm her son's maleness, and usually a parental couple who together are able to acknowledge and love their son. These primary object experiences come alive in our male patients' transferences as well as in our corresponding countertransferences when we find ourselves inhabiting these parental role-based positions in both their positive and negative polarities.

Let's briefly consider each of these while keeping in mind that though the focus is on traditional heterosexual coupling, these triadic parenting issues also pertain to homosexual couples where the partner who is more of the "second" other is called upon to draw the primary nurturer back into their sexual liaison. Each partner's initial identifications with their own feminine and masculine caretakers play a significant role in these dynamics as implied in my subsequent discussion pertaining to the "'father' in the 'mother'" (and vice versa). However, it is beyond the scope of this chapter to discuss homosexual and single-parenting in more detail.

The involved father

The father plays an important role in the establishment of his son's gender identity within the early triadic relationship, as Freud (1921) observed. Freud also wrote of the boy's early love for his father and the ubiquity of psychic bisexuality (see Freud, 1925). In furthering Freud's insights, several post-Freudian analysts have incisively conceptualised the dyadic, early father-son relationship and the triangular dynamics of the rapprochement phase wherein both parents need to contain and manage their own separation issues and competitive, envious feelings (e.g., Abelin, 1971, 1975, 1980; Benjamin, 1988, 1991; Blos, 1984). In the little boy's turning away from, and experiencing loss in relationship to, his mother, an available, preoedipal father as "the second other" (Greenspan, 1982) tempers his son's more defensive tendencies to disengage forcefully from her while providing a conventional focus for masculine identification (Diamond, 1998; 2004b). The boy who is able to achieve a reciprocal identification with an available, loving father who possesses a body and genitalia like his own—who is like the boy but who remains independent and outside the boy's control—facilitates his son's integration of his maternal-feminine identifications by making possible the internalisation of a paternal imago (representing genital masculinity) in which the active and penetrating *as well as* the receptive and caretaking qualities of the father's parenting become a foundation for healthy masculine gender identity.

The parental couple

The boy's internalisation of this healthy, genital father imago also depends on the nature of the father's relationship to the mother, and hers with the father. A mother experiences dramatic shifts in her libidinal life that typically begin during pregnancy and continue when her attunement to her baby is dominant (cf. Winnicott, 1956). For that reason, a father is frequently called upon to invite his wife to return to their conjugal relationship so that she learns to divide more of her focus between the maternal and spousal parts of herself.

By drawing his wife back to him, particularly as her son initially begins to separate from her, the father protects both the marriage's adult sexuality and intimacy and facilitates his son's efforts to differentiate from his primary object. Hence, in using his libido to strengthen his connection with his wife, a father offers his child an object of identification able to locate maleness within the matrix of intimate relationship (Herzog, 2005b). This sexual bond between parents provides the child with, in Winnicott's (1964) words, "a rock to which he can cling and against which he can kick" (p. 115).

By being both a *caring father* to his son and an *exciting lover* to his wife, a father helps his little boy place the *primary couple* together in "triangular space" (Britton, 1989; see also Bollas, 2000; Britton, 1999; Klein, 1945;). The preoedipal triadic reality of being jointly regarded by his parents rather than individually appropriated by either for their unconscious need fulfilment, generates a more favourable oedipal phase (Herzog, 2005a).

The attuned mother

A mother's recognition and affirmation of her son's maleness helps him to progressively differentiate from her rather than to establish his sense of masculinity in violent opposition to her femaleness. This entails the mother's support for her son's journey toward the world of his father—the world of males. Needless to say, the mother's separation anxieties and oedipal dynamics are crucial, for she has to be able to modulate her own competitive and envious impulses as they emerge during this early period of triangulation.

A son who is not supported by his mother when he is turning outwards from her tends to internalise a particular identification with her—one that in effect opposes his "phallic" forays toward his father and the external world. This problematic identification then operates to impede a boy's healthy aggression, competition, mastery, and authority—as if these qualities would themselves represent an attack on the mother.

The little boy's maternal identifications—the "father" in the "mother"

The mother's endorsing her son as a male person tends to operate more unconsciously, and her boy identifies with these unconscious attitudes— what Ogden (1989) calls the paradox of "masculinity-in-femininity". His sense of masculinity is especially impacted by his mother's feelings about his physicality, sensuality, and temperament as well as by her endorsement of the father's paternal authority, and little boys lacking this recognition establish a highly conflictual internalisation of their mothers. For these boys, particularly when their fathers are emotionally or physically absent, phallic narcissism becomes psychically urgent and the "narcissistically valorized" penis (Braunschweig & Fain, 1993) is used defensively, often featuring perverse sexuality (see Herzog, 2004).

For example, Brad, a thirty-something patient of mine, whose father abandoned the family and whose mother was "burdened" by her son's maleness, spent month after month in therapy recounting his daily sexual conquests while attributing his "successes" to the enormous size of his penis and his gigantic, brilliant mind. Indeed, the phallocentric male operates defensively, as if his phallus is all that he has to make him masculine. Interestingly, Brad's analytic work could truly begin only when, to his dismay, he found himself romantically involved with a transsexual partner and thus was forced to examine his defensively constructed, highly fragile sense of masculinity.

The gendered nature of the male's ego ideal

So how are we to understand the shaping of the boy's ego ideal along gendered lines, or to put it more colloquially, why is the "male ego" so important for men (see Diamond, 2006, 2009)? In short, I believe that the gendered nature of the masculine ego ideal is founded on the boy's distinctive struggles during the initial stages of gender differentiation— a struggle requiring the little boy to adapt to a significant disruption in relation to his mother. It is the boy's gendered ego ideal that helps him to heal what he experiences as an abrupt, rather traumatic sense of loss during his struggle to separate from her.

The boy's separation "trauma" and the male's sense of shame

Psychoanalysts have cast the boy's experience of separating from his mother's world as his initial preoedipal crisis, or "trauma", wherein he must adapt to the loss just as he is realising that he is sexually different from his mother—a veritable "traumatic discovery of otherness" (Ogden, 1989). Thus, this loss occurs as he realises that he can neither be the mother nor be of her female gender; Lax (1997) regards this "painful narcissistic mortification" (p. 118) as the bedrock trauma for males.

The boy not only loses a large part of his primary dyadic connection, but is also pressured to repudiate what he has lost. Normative socialisation for males relies heavily on the aversive power of shame to shape acceptable male behaviour. For example, little boys are pressured to renounce gender-inconsistent traits far more than young girls are (see Fast, 1984; Hansell, 1998) and taboos against cross-gender behaviour tend to be enforced much more brutally by parents, peers, and the society generally when exhibited by boys (see Maccoby, 1998). There are also greater prohibitions against early homoerotic attachments and homosexuality for boys, including their father-directed erotic desires, in addition to their early maternal erotic attachment (Wrye & Welles, 1994). Basically, boys do *not* grow up experiencing themselves as masculine by dint of being male; masculinity has to be won and typically proven repeatedly.

The gender-related issue of being independent from his mother—rather than (in English language insults) a "momma's boy", "tied to her apron strings", or a "pussy, sissy, or faggot", let alone (and God forbid!) a "mother fucker"—reinforces his need to conform. Owing to this culturally enforced aspect of his separation from the mother-orbit, the young boy may feel emotionally abandoned without being aware of it (see Pollack, 1998), while experiencing his identification with his mother as shameful. As we see with adult males, this is often manifest in defensive efforts against neediness in an effort to stave off shame states (see Elise, 2001 in her discussion of these "impenetrable citadels").

Phallic narcissism and maturing masculinity

As Freud indicated, phallic narcissism begins as a natural, adaptive process to mitigate the small boy's experience of loss and envy. The boy's traumatic loss of the "paradise" of the earliest, highly gratifying relationship with his mother disposes him to create a phallic image of himself in relation to the world in order to regain control of the object now experienced as quite separate from his ego (Chasseguet-Smirgel, 1976, 1984, 1985; Manninen, 1992, 1993). In other words, the male's heroic quest commences as the little boy's phallic image provides him with an illusory way to win his mother's love.

The phallus partially represents the lost breast as his penis replaces the breast as the superior organ. In turn, the boy's breast envy is relegated to the deeper unconscious (Lax, 1997). The little boy omnipotently forms the adaptive and defensive illusion of "the supremacy of his own masculine equipment" (Manninen, 1992, p. 25), and the phallus, initially employed to assuage the boy's differentiation anxieties, becomes the symbol of invulnerability—a permanently erect monolith of masculine omnipotence (Ducat, 2004)—manically defending against the depressive dangers of an all-too separate but still needed maternal object. In short, phallic monism—the belief that the penis is *the* sexual organ—comes to guard against any recognition of lack or deficiency.

The phallic ego ideal is thus based on the boy's unconscious denial of differentiation in the service of his grandiose wish for maintaining the unlimited possibility inherent in the omnipotent, idealised union with his maternal object. The seminal issue for most men is how this early, preoedipal phallic narcissism and phallic omnipotence becomes integrated into an ongoing and evolving sense of masculinity (Diamond, 2004a, 2006, 2009).

However, for some men without an opportunity for a maturing ego ideal that integrates the phallic ego ideal with the genital ego ideal, a hypermasculine image of manhood becomes largely compensatory and constitutes a narcissistic end in itself, for example in the constant urge to assert oneself impressively, rather than serve more creative purposes (Schalin, 1989). True differentiation is denied while penetration offers the promise of transcendence of vulnerability, limitation, and dependence.

This arrested phallic narcissism or *defensive phallicity*—in contrast to the more *adaptive phallicity* with its suitable penile pride that fuels creative, purposeful activity in childhood, adolescence and, particularly, in young adulthood—ultimately becomes a persistent obstacle to maturing adult development and is evident both in the *fragmentation anxieties* and the sense of *shame* that are evoked whenever a stable masculine identity *cannot* be maintained. Healthy phallicism is based primarily on what classical psychoanalysis refers to as neutralisation, sublimation, and integration of the grandiose strivings of phallic-narcissism or exhibitionism as well as phallic omnipotence during the oedipal phase (Edgcumbe & Burgner, 1975; Schalin, 1983). This phallic development occurs mainly because of involved, good enough fathering (or surrogate fathering) during a son's preoedipal, oedipal, and latency years. Other analysts have also distinguished the healthy, adaptive nature of phallic narcissism from the pathologically defensive type, especially by emphasising the importance of the bodily component in the desire to penetrate (see Corbett, 2003; Schalin, 1989).

Many men experience this as a psychic, life-and-death struggle, as the Pulitzer Prize winning poet, Stephen Dunn (2004) poignantly conveys in "Achilles in Love":

> There was *no getting to his weakness.*
> *In public*, even in summer, he wore big boots, especially made for him,
> a band of steel reinforcing each heel.
> *At home*, when he bathed or slept, he kept a pistol within reach, loaded.
> And because *to be invulnerable is to be alone*, he was *alone when he was with you.*
> You could sense it in the rigidity of his carriage, as if under his fine-fitting suits were *layers of armor.* …
> Then she came along, who seemed to be all women fused into one, …
> You could see his body soften, and days later, when *finally they were naked*,
> she instinctively knew what to do …
> —*kiss his heel before kissing what he considered to be his power,*
> and with *a tenderness that made him tremble.*
> …
> And so *Achilles began to live differently.*
> Both friends and enemies were astounded by h*is willingness to listen, and hesitate* before responding. Even in victory *he'd walk away without angering* a single god.
> He wore sandals now because she liked him in sandals.
> *He never felt so exposed, or so open* to the world.
> You could see in his face something resembling *terror*,
> But in fact it was love, for which *he would die.* (pp. 66–67, italics added)

Transforming masculinity in the course of male development

The relationship between these phallic facets and the genital features of a man's masculinity is continually being reworked, evoking distinct challenges at key developmental junctures. These challenges emerge for a male largely with respect to his actual and symbolic father, particularly during the oedipal and latency phases, in adolescence and young adulthood, and again during mid- and later life. For example, during his oedipal phase and latency years, a boy's sense of his masculinity is especially impacted by his father's beneficial use of his paternal authority, emotional regulatory capacity (particularly in modulating aggression), and admirable skill in doing things. The boy's sense of his maleness, then, is directly related to his budding ability to express and modulate aggressive and competitive urges, acquire a sense of industry, and attenuate his adaptively needed, albeit illusionary, phallic omnipotence. In adolescence, as the boy differentiates from his family in seeking to develop his own identity, his masculinity is considerably influenced by his father's capacity to bear his son's moving away from him (as the boy did earlier with his mother) and constructively deal with the threats to his own narcissism, as well as by the teenage peer group's sanctioning of his masculine identity. Accordingly, by late adolescence and early adulthood, a young man's sense of manhood is directly tied to adult identity formation, especially influenced by his sexual prowess and ability to endure pain. In young adulthood, mentors are crucial as the young man embarks on his "heroic" journey to become his "own man" with lasting intimate relationships in the world outside his family. Thus, during his adult years, he is more likely to appraise his manhood in terms of his career success and ability to provide for and relate to his family. Finally, in his mid- and later life, undoubtedly related to the diminishment of testosterone, his manliness becomes more flexible, typically in the course of evaluating the success of his generativity and, most likely, fatherliness. Moreover, throughout these developmental transitions, the interior phallic and genital positions become anchored in particular ego ideals during young, middle, and later adulthood.

Reworking the balance between phallic and genital ego ideals in aging

Of foremost clinical significance is the fact that adult men who are able to develop a maturing ego ideal that integrates the phallic ego ideal with the genital ego ideal, are freed from their reliance on the bifurcated, "phallicised" manhood that plays such an important, beneficial role during men's childhood, youthful, and younger adult adaptations.

The achievement of a mature sense of masculine identity depends on the adequate negotiation of a shifting balance between the phallic ego ideal and the genital ego ideal through the life cycle.

In early adulthood, men attempt to live up to idealised notions of what it is to be a man, notions that are reminiscent of the phallic little boy's view of his father. Thus, young adult men are typically dominated by the phallic ego ideal characterised by the "heroic illusion" (Axelrod, 1997). However, they increasingly need to call upon more of a genital ego ideal to establish lasting, intimate relationships, and if all goes well, grandiosity lessens, a sense of otherness and empathy increases, and maturing adulthood is on course.

By midlife, a man's changing masculinity optimally weighs the perpetual male struggle more along "genital" lines, as the pleasures of receptivity, being, experiencing, and understanding frequently come to take precedence over the excitement of striving and reaching, and priority is given to insight, connection, and nurturance. For biological and psychological reasons, the aging man is forced to deal with the dismantling of male certitude, most forcibly in the arena of gender identity. There is a "necessity of growing small" (Manninen, 1992, p. 23)—namely, less grandiose, omnipotent, phallic—in order to become "whole", and the ideals previously associated with *becoming a man* give way to those associated with *becoming a person*.

By achieving the ability to enjoy being a man without disavowing identifications with women, many men reconcile their new definition of what it means to be a man with the more rigid notion of masculinity formed early on (Diamond, 2004a). For others, it is only in old age, if ever, that the object dependence of human existence, "the first fact of life", is no longer denied while the illusory Western attitude of autonomous individuality is finally overcome and our fundamental relational nature fully embraced (Teising, 2008).

In closing we can hear the more flexible, less gendered male ego ideal reflecting a well-integrated phallic and genital interior space in Walt Whitman's (1855) timeless ode of fully realised manhood (from *Leaves of Grass*):

> I am of old and young, of the foolish as much as the wise,
> Regardless of others, ever regardful of others,
> Maternal as well as paternal, a child as well as a man.
>   (p. 40, (16), 326–328)

References

Abelin, E. L. (1971). The role of the father in the separation-individuation process. In: J. B. McDevitt & C. F. Settlage (Eds.), *Separation-Individuation* (pp. 229–252). NY: International Universities Press.

Abelin, E. L. (1975). Some further observations and comments on the earliest role of the father. *International Journal of Psychoanalysis, 56*: 293–302.

Abelin, E. L. (1980). Triangulation, the role of the father and the origins of core gender identity during the rapprochement subphase. In: R. F. Lax, S. Bach & J. A. Burland (Eds.), *Rapprochement* (pp. 151–170). New York: Aronson.

Axelrod, S. D. (1997). Developmental pathways to masculinity: A reconsideration of Greenson's "Disidentifying from Mother". *Issues in Psychoanalytic Psychology, 19*: 101–115.

Balint, M. (1948). On genital love. *International Journal of Psychoanalysis, 29*: 34–40.

Baron-Cohen, S. (2003). *The Essential Difference: The Truth About the Male and Female Brain*. New York: Basic Books.

Benjamin, J. (1988). *The Bonds of Love*. NY: Pantheon Books.

Benjamin, J. (1991). Father and daughter: Identification with a difference—a contribution to gender heterodoxy. *Psychoanalytic Dialogues, 1*: 277–299.

Benjamin, J. (1996). *Gender and Psychoanalysis*. Madison, CT: International Universities Press.

Bion, W. R. (1965). *Transformations: Change from Learning to Growth*. London: Tavistock.

Bion, W. R. (1970). *Attention and Interpretation: A Scientific Approach to Insight in Psycho-Analysis and Groups*. London: Tavistock.

Blos, P. (1984). Son and father. *Journal of the American Psychoanalytic Association, 32*: 301–324.

Bollas, C. (2000). *Hysteria*. New York: Routledge.

Bordo, S. (1999). *The Male Body*. New York: Farrar, Straus & Giroux.

Brady, M. T. (2006). The riddle of masculinity. *Journal of the American Psychoanalytic Association, 4*: 1195–1206.

Braunschweig, D. & Fain, M. (1993). The phallic shadow. In: D. Breen (Ed.), *The Gender Conundrum* (pp. 130–144). London: Routledge.

Britton, R. (1989). The missing link: parental sexuality in the Oedipus complex. In: J. Steiner (Ed.), *The Oedipus Complex Today* (pp. 83–102). London: Karnac.

Britton, R. (1999). Getting in on the act: The hysterical solution. *International Journal of Psychoanalysis, 80*: 1–13.

Campbell, D. (1995). The role of the father in a pre-suicide state. *International Journal of Psychoanalysis, 76*: 315–323.

Chasseguet-Smirgel, J. (1976). Freud and female sexuality: The consideration of some blind spots in the exploration of the "Dark Continent". *International Journal of Psychoanalysis, 57*: 275–286.

Chasseguet-Smirgel, J. (1984). *Creativity and Perversion*. New York: Norton.

Chasseguet-Smirgel, J. (1985). *The Ego Ideal*. New York: Norton.

Corbett, K. (2003). Pride/Power/Penis. Paper Presented at the Spring meeting of the Division of Psychoanalysis (39) of the American Psychological Association, Minneapolis, MN, April, 2003.

De Simone Gaburri, G. (1985). On termination of the analysis. *International Review of Psychoanalysis, 12*: 461–468.

Diamond, M. J. (1997). Boys to men: The maturing of masculine gender identity through paternal watchful protectiveness. *Gender and Psychoanalysis, 2*: 443–468.

Diamond, M. J. (1998). Fathers with sons: Psychoanalytic perspectives on "good enough" fathering throughout the life cycle. *Gender and Psychoanalysis, 3*: 243–299.

Diamond, M. J. (2004a). Accessing the multitude within: A psychoanalytic perspective on the transformation of masculinity at mid-life. *International Journal of Psychoanalysis, 85*: 45–64.

Diamond, M. J. (2004b). The shaping of masculinity: Revisioning boys turning away from their mothers to construct male gender identity. *International Journal of Psychoanalysis, 85*: 359–380.

Diamond, M. J. (2006). Masculinity unraveled: The roots of male gender identity and the shifting of male ego ideals throughout life. *Journal of the American Psychoanalytic Association, 4*: 1099–1130.

Diamond, M. J. (2007). *My Father Before Me: How Fathers and Sons Influence Each Other Throughout Their Lives*. New York: W. W. Norton.

Diamond, M. J. (2009). Masculinity and its discontents: Making room for the "mother" inside the male—an essential achievement for healthy male gender identity. In: B. Reis & R. Grossmark's (Eds.), *Heterosexual Masculinities* (pp. 23–53). New York: Analytic Press.

Ducat, S. J. (2004). *The Wimp Factor: Gender Gaps, Holy Wars, & the Politics of Anxious Masculinity*. Boston, MA: Beacon Press.

Dunn, S. (2004). Achilles in Love. In: *The Insistence of Beauty* (pp. 66–67). New York: W. W. Norton.

Edgcumbe, R. & Burgner, M. (1975). The phallic-narcissistic phase. *The Psychoanalytic Study of the Child, 30*: 161–180.

Elise, D. (2001). Unlawful entry: Male fears of psychic penetration. *Psychoanalytic Dialogues, 11*: 499–531.

Fast, I. (1984). Gender *Identity*. Hillsdale, NJ: Analytic Press.

Fast, I. (1990). Aspects of early gender development: Toward a reformulation. *Psychoanalytic Psychology, 7 (Suppl.)*: 105–117.

Fast, I. (1999). Aspects of core gender identity. *Psychoanalytic Dialogues*, 9: 633–661.

Ferenczi, S. (1924). *Thalassa: A Theory of Genitality*. London, Karnac, 1989.

Figlio, K. (2010). Phallic and seminal masculinity: A theoretical and clinical confusion. *International Journal of Psychoanalysis*, 91: 119–139.

Fogel, G. I. (1998). Interiority and inner genital space in men: What else can be lost in castration? *Psychoanalytic Quarterly*, 67: 662–697.

Fogel, G. I. (2006). Riddles of masculinity: Gender, bisexuality, and thirdness. *Journal of the American Psychoanalytic Association*, 4: 1139–1163.

Fonagy, P. (2001). *Attachment Theory and Psychoanalysis*. New York: Other Press.

Freud, S. (1905). Three essays on the theory of sexuality. *S. E.*, 7: 125–243. London: Hogarth.

Freud, S. (1921). Group psychology and the analysis of the ego. *S. E.*, 18: 69–143. London: Hogarth.

Freud, S. (1923). The infantile genital organization: an interpolation into the theory of sexuality. *S. E.*, 19: 140–145. London: Hogarth.

Freud, S. (1924). The dissolution of the Oedipus complex. *S. E.*, 19: 173–179. London: Hogarth.

Freud, S. (1925). Some psychological consequences of the anatomical differences between the sexes. *S. E.*, 19: 248–258. London: Hogarth.

Freud, S. (1937). Analysis terminable and interminable. *S. E.*, 23: 209–254. London: Hogarth.

Friedman, R. (1996). The role of the testicles in male psychological development. *Journal of the American Psychoanalytic Association*, 44: 201–253.

Gilmore, D. D. (1990). *Manhood in the Making*. New Haven, CT: Yale University Press.

Greenson, R. R. (1966). A transsexual boy and a hypothesis. *International Journal of Psychoanalysis*, 47: 396–403.

Greenson, R. R. (1968). Disidentifying from mother: Its special importance for the boy. *International Journal of Psychoanalysis*, 49: 370–374.

Greenspan, S. I. (1982). "The second other": The role of the father in early personality formation and the dyadic-phallic phase of development. In: S. H. Cath, A. R. Gurwitt & J. M. Ross (Eds.), *Father and Child: Developmental and Clinical Perspectives* (pp. 123–138). Boston: Little, Brown and Co.

Hansell, J. H. (1998). Gender anxiety, gender melancholia, gender perversion. *Psychoanalytic Dialogues*, 8: 337–351.

Harris, A. (1991). Gender as contradiction. *Psychoanalytic Dialogues*, 1: 197–224.

Heidigger, M. (1959). *Discourse on Thinking: A Translation of Gelassenheit* (J. M. Anderson & E. H. Freund, Trans.). New York: Harper and Row, 1969.

Herzog, J. M. (2004). Father hunger and narcissistic deformation. *Psychoanalytic Quarterly, 73*: 893–914.
Herzog, J. M. (2005a). Triadic reality and the capacity to love. *Psychoanalytic Quarterly, 74*: 1029–1052.
Herzog, J. M. (2005b). What fathers do and how they do it. In: S. F. Brown (Ed.), *What Do Mothers Want?* (pp. 55–68). Hillsdale, NJ: The Analytic Press.
Jones, E. (1933). The phallic phase. *International Journal of Psychoanalysis, 14*: 1–33.
Keats, J. (1817). From a letter to George and Thomas Keats, December 21, 1817. In: J. P. Hunter (Ed.), *The Norton Introduction to Literature: The Poetry* (pp. 477–478). New York: W. W. Norton, 1973.
Kestenberg, J. (1968). Outside and inside: Male and female. *Journal of the American Psychoanalytic Association, 16*: 457–520.
Klein, M. (1945). The Oedipus complex in light of early anxieties. In: *The Writings of Melanie Klein, Volume 3* (pp. 370–419). New York: Free Press.
Kulish, N. (2010). Clinical implications of contemporary gender theory. *Journal of the American Psychoanalytic Association, 58*: 231–258.
Labouvie-Vief, G. (1994). *Psyche and Eros: Mind and Gender in the Life Course.* Cambridge: Cambridge University Press.
Lax, R. F. (1997). Boys' envy of mother and the consequences of this narcissistic mortification. *The Psychoanalytic Study of the Child, 52*: 118–139.
Loewald, H. W. (1962). Internalization, separation, mourning, and the superego. *Psychoanalytic Quarterly, 31*: 483–504.
Lyons-Ruth, K. (1991). Rapprochement or approchement: Mahler's theory reconsidered from the vantage point of recent research in early attachment relationships. *Psychoanalytic Psychology, 8*: 1–23.
Maccoby, E. E. (1998). The *Two Sexes: Growing Apart, Coming Together.* Cambridge, MA: Harvard University Press.
Mahler, M. S., Pine, F. & Bergman, A. (1975). *The Psychological Birth of the Human Infant: Symbiosis and Individuation.* New York: Basic Books.
Manninen, V. (1992). The ultimate masculine striving: Reflexions on the psychology of two polar explorers. *Scandinavian Psychoanalytic Review, 15*: 1–26.
Manninen, V. (1993). For the sake of eternity: On the narcissism of fatherhood and the father-son relationship. *Scandinavian Psychoanalytic Review, 16*: 35–46.
Ogden, T. H. (1989). The *Primitive Edge of Experience.* Northvale, NJ: Aronson.
Panksepp, J. (1998). *Affective Neuroscience: The Foundations of Human and Animal Emotions.* New York: Oxford University Press.

Person, E. S. (2006). Masculinities, plural. *Journal of the American Psychoanalytic Association*, 4: 1165–1186.

Pollack, W. S. (1995). Deconstructing dis-identification: Rethinking psychoanalytic concepts of male development. *Psychoanalysis and Psychotherapy*, 12: 30–45.

Pollack, W. S. (1998). *Real Boys: Rescuing Our Sons from the Myths of Boyhood*. New York: Random House.

Reis, B. (2008). Names of the father. In: B. Reis & R. Grossmark (Eds.), Heterosexual *Masculinities* (pp. 55–72). New York: Analytic Press.

Schalin, L. J. (1983). Phallic integration and male identity development: Aspects on the importance of the father relation to boys in the latency period. *Scandinavian Psychoanalytic Review*, 6: 21–42.

Schalin, L. J. (1989). On phallicism: Developmental aspects, neutralization, sublimation and defensive phallicism. *Scandinavian Psychoanalytic Review*, 12: 38–57.

Stoller, R. (1964). A contribution to the study of gender identity. *International Journal of Psychoanalysis*, 45: 220–226.

Stoller, R. (1965). The sense of maleness. *Psychoanalytic Quarterly*. 34: 207–218.

Stoller, R. (1968). Sex *and Gender, Vol. 1: The Development of Masculinity and Femininity*. London: Hogarth Press.

Stoller, R. (1976). Primary femininity. *Journal of the American Psychoanalytic Association*, 24: 59–78.

Teising, M. (2008). At life's end—between narcissistic denial and the facts of life. Unpublished manuscript.

Whitman, W. (1855/1986). *Leaves of Grass*. New York: Penguin (Orig. published in 1855).

Winnicott, D. W. (1956). Primary maternal preoccupation. In: *Collected Papers: Through Pediatrics to Psycho-Analysis*, (pp. 300–305). New York: Basic Books 1958.

Winnicott, D. W. (1964). *The Child, the Family and the Outside World*. New York: Penguin Books.

Wrye, H. & Welles, J. K. (1994). *The Narration of Desire: Erotic Transferences and Countertransferences*. Hillsdale, NJ: Analytic Press.

Young-Eisendrath, P. (1997). Gender and contrasexuality: Jung's contribution and beyond. In: P. Young-Eisendrath & T. Dawson (Eds.), *The Cambridge Companion to Jung* (pp. 223–239). Cambridge: Cambridge University Press.

CHAPTER TWO

Discussion of "Evolving perspectives on masculinity and its discontents: reworking the internal phallic and genital positions"*

Giovanna Ambrosio

I should like to begin by thanking Michael Diamond for the many stimulating points that he presents.

It is not easy for me to discuss a theoretical work that is so well organised and meaningful. Furthermore, I am in agreement with Diamond on many aspects of his paper; first among them, the attention that he gives to the very early levels of development and the constant distinction that he makes between phallic and genital, the non-linearity of their development, and the co-existence of different areas. It is never easy to "detach" clinical work from theory since, considering the nature of psychoanalysis, they are inseparable. When faced with a theoretical paper so full of content, it would be especially important to focus our discussion also on the clinical material, and I felt that this was lacking in this paper.

What characterises the psychoanalytic concepts is closely connected to, and will depend on, the overall implicit and explicit theory of every psychoanalyst. Due to the fact that perhaps Diamond and I do not share the same theoretical background, it was very interesting and

---

*Translated by Jill Whitelaw-Cucco.

constructive for me to compare the differences in the way we deal with these issues. We could discuss, at length, many aspects that emerge from this paper; I will, however, focus on a few short counterpoints.

Consideration of the early levels of psychic development

The question that I ask is the following: when we speak of very early levels, are we all referring to the same thing? What do we include under the "umbrella" of the term "early levels" or preoedipal levels?

Within our theory, there are numerous models that are different from one another (the four psychologies, as Pine (1988) calls them), each with its own particular description. In *drive psychology*, the initial crux lies in the conflict relative to the danger of desire and to its resolution, whereas for *ego psychology* the individual is considered in terms of the slow and linear capacity for adaptation, with a continuous dialectic interplay between reality testing and defences. For *object relations psychology*—particularly the Kleinian model—from the very beginning there is the interplay of relations, even though between partial objects, and therefore always in the context of drives; while for *self psychology*, and Winnicott in particular, the term preoedipal indicates a pre-object and pre-drive phase. Thus, the main focus is on the degree of differentiation of self from other, on the sense of separateness, and on setting of boundaries.

There is not space here to refer to the many and different important authors; however, whatever our theoretical model of reference may be, I think that we would all agree to distinguish—and not only quantitatively—primitive levels such as imitation, primary identification, projective identification, undifferentiation, distinction between self and not-self, from the subsequent levels of identity resulting from the endless process of introjection, structurisation, and integration.

Following the thoughts of Winnicott and Greenacre, Gaddini (1977) formulated the hypothesis of a process of development that is not linear, but in which different areas co-exist that can take precedence over each other according to the vicissitudes of the intra—and inter-psychic life of the individual. In particular, he described two areas of mental functioning within the first self-object relational vicissitudes that, in some way, persist throughout life. The more archaic *psycho-sensorial* area is linked to very early bodily experiences, giving the illusion of "being the object" through contact, at the service of an omnipotent, fusional and non-conflictual phase; while the *psycho-oral* area, linked to "having the object" through incorporation-introjection, within a self-object relation, is more drive-oriented (this is dealt with more thoroughly in classical theory) and is where conflict and dependence come to the forefront.

Our different ways of understanding the concept of disidentification

And so, what do we mean by disidentification? Speaking of real identification involves the already complex vicissitudes of the organisation and structurisation of identity. For us analysts, this is a complicated concept that, in its turn, contains other concepts such as incorporation, imitation, projective identification, adhesive identification, introjection. For years, the complexity of this concept has been the theme of theoretical discussions and critical reviews according to the different models of reference.

The first time that Freud made public his concept of identification and discussed it was in *The Interpretation of Dreams* regarding the "psychic contamination" he had noticed in hysteria. He wrote: "Identification is not, therefore, merely imitation, but assimilation on the basis of a presumed etiological similarity. It expresses a resemblance and derives from a common element, that remains unconscious" (1900, p. x). In another work he defined primary identification as "the earliest affective bond with another person; in these primary identifications the ego copies the person" (Freud, 1921). For Freud, primary identification was a form belonging "to the pre-history of the Oedipus", direct and immediate, that does not involve object investment. Secondary identifications, on the other hand, a later and structurising development, were to his mind the result of the introjective processes at the time of the resolution of the Oedipal complex. In other words, a primary identification in which the infant imitates in order "to be" the mother; a secondary identification that allows him to reach the stage of "having" the mother.

Many eminent analysts—Fenichel, Ferenczi, Deutsch, Greenacre, Greenson, Stoller, and Gaddini—have distinguished imitative phenomena from what could seem to be identification. Referring to these very early levels, Jacobson spoke of "first identifications". However, identifying oneself necessarily implies the possibility of introjecting and (as Freud said) assimilating reality, even though in a fragmentary way (Gaddini, 1968). Also Winnicott (1956) said that primary identification indicates an environment that is still undifferentiated.

Unlike identifications, imitations have to do with the unconscious fantasy; they are connected to bodily sensations, to primitive perceptions, to a phase in which there is as yet no boundary between inside and outside, in which the object is not perceived as such but as part of the self.

Greenson's case of Lance, to which Diamond refers, is not, to my mind, an example of a case of lack of disidentification, but a case of non-achievement of individuation and therefore of identification. It is a paradigmatic example of the prevalence of an imitative area. Greenson says that when Lance "played with a lorry … he became the lorry"; and from Greenson's account, as well as the interesting summary of Stoller, who had Lance's mother in analysis, it emerged that the child had for a long time been in a state of oneness with the mother's body: he *was* the mother. Therefore, imitation precedes the structurisation of identification of which it is a component together with introjection.

Having said this, how can we speak of disidentification if there has not yet been identification? Following the thoughts of analysts such as Winnicott, Gaddini, Amati Mehler, and Argentieri, I prefer to think in terms of undifferentation and, therefore—in clinical work—in terms of process of separation, differentiation, and individuation.

The process of the primal scene

During the course of the primal scene process, considered as a ubiquitous process (Greenacre, Gaddini) that accompanies the whole development of the child, the figure of the father as second object is initially a confused copy that evokes a strange and deformed maternal image; the putting into focus of a second object that is distinct and separate will be slow and gradual and requires first of all the recognition of an external mother.

Therefore, in order to become individuals, boys and girls first have to separate and differentiate themselves from the primary fusional situation with the mother, experienced in turn as being not differentiated from the father, until—through the vicissitudes of the Oedipus and the primal scene—they reach the stage of confronting the father as "second object" (Argentieri, 1985; Gaddini, 1977) who is distinct and differentiated from the mother.

We could say that the acquisition of a balanced "thirdness" and therefore of the second object—paradigm of the possibility to "become" and to accede to otherness—is the substance of the psychoanalytic process co-related to drive interplay.

Of course, it is very important to distinguish on one hand mother and father as concrete persons, and on the other hand the maternal and paternal function transmissible from generation to generation.

Masculine and feminine vicissitudes

In the essay to which Diamond refers—"Disidentifying from mother— Its special importance for the boy"—Greenson (1968) writes, regarding the little boy: "(He) must replace the primary object of his identification, the mother, and must identify instead with the father". (p. 370). Concerning the little girl, he writes: "The girl too must dis-identify from mother if she is to develop her own unique identity, but her identification with mother *helps* her to establish her own feminine identity" (p. 370).

We might, however, ask ourselves whether, for the little girl, it is not just as complicated, if not more so, to differentiate herself from mother's body and then, in the future, have to identify again with it. In contrast with what Greenson (1968) and many other authors after him have maintained, I believe that the identification of the little girl with the mother does not help her to establish her femininity. What is more, the primary undifferentiated fusional situation can more easily help towards an imitative pseudo-femininity. In the same way, growing up and becoming a woman (i.e., bodily the same as the mother) for the little girl could mean "being" the mother, thus facilitating a regression towards that fusional primary bond that prevents the establishment of her own identity.

Fajrajzen (1973), in his attempt to explain why woman are "more symbiotic" than men, wrote that in his opinion men have gone further in their separation-individuation processes because in their effort to separate from the mother, they tend to develop their aggressive drives more.

Which love?

In "On the universal tendency to debasement in the sphere of love", Freud (1912), writing about masculine impotence, claims that

> the foundation of the disorder is provided by an inhibition in the developmental history of the libido before it assumes the form

which we take to be its normal termination .... An incestuous fixation ... plays a prominent part in this pathogenic material and is its
most universal content .... Two currents, whose union is necessary
to ensure a completely normal attitude in love have, in the cases we
are considering, failed to combine. These two may be distinguished
as the affectionate and the sensual current. (p. 180)

As Amati Mehler (1992) reminds us in her paper on "Love and male
impotence", "When affection and sensuality are not linked but opposed,
due to fixation to incestuous fantasies, the capacity to love will be
marked by this split. The sensual current and the sexual wish can only
seek gratification from two different objects since fusion of both currents has failed" (p. 467).

In agreement with Amati Mehler (I refer also to her paper "The abyss
of intimacy", this volume), and in line with the thinking of Winnicott
and Gaddini, I believe that it is fundamental to distinguish the two concepts of sensuality and sexuality. Sensuality is connected with pleasure
provided by sense organs. In this way we could say that sensuality in the
form of tender and exciting contact belongs to the area of needs; it corresponds to a guarantee of the survival of the self—therefore of "being".
Sexuality, which in its more mature, genital expressions includes sensuality as the earliest phase of "affection", regards the area of object relations, of desire—an area that is exquisitely drive-oriented and requires
a quota of healthy aggressiveness, and is therefore conflictual.

Concerning this point, I should like to refer to Diamond's patient,
Brad—a case about which it would be interesting to know more—whose
"analytic work could truly begin only when, to his dismay, he found
himself romantically involved with a transsexual partner and thus was
forced to examine his defensively constructed, highly fragile sense of
masculinity". We may think of him as being a patient who, thanks to
the transference, is able to renounce his imitative pseudo-genitality,
regressing to a tender and romantic quality with an undifferentiated
person, but still a long way from being able to integrate sensuality with
sexuality, or tender exciting contact with drive vicissitudes.

The focal point, when we are speaking about male and/or female
sexuality, remains how the oedipal and preoedipal levels interact with
each other: how does the meeting between Narcissus and Oedipus
occur? How have the first defence organisations been articulated

regarding archaic anxieties of integration-non integration, of loss of self and of annihilation?

It is important to consider how successive stages of growth have been conditioned by what has happened before; but also, through a "retroactive resignification", how the "after" reorganises and reconstitutes the meaning of "before".

In the analytic situation, it is fundamental to understand this, and also in relation to the type of interpretation to make. In fact, it is not always easy to keep in view our tendency to interpret one level rather than another, thus losing sight of the crucial point that is precisely the intersection between the very early representations of the self that are in need of fusion, and the conflicts that follow the separation between self and object.

Development or regression?

One final observation regarding the last paragraph of Diamond's "Reworking the balance between phallic and genital ego ideals in aging". He writes: "There is a 'necessity of growing small'—namely, less grandiose, omnipotent, phallic—in order to become 'whole', and the ideals previously associated with *becoming a man* give way to those associated with *becoming a person*". He continues: "For others, it is only in old age, if ever, that the object dependence of human existence, 'the first fact of life', is no longer denied while the illusory Western attitude of autonomous individuality is finally overcome and our fundamental relational nature fully embraced".

In my opinion, however, *becoming a person*, as well as the passage from pathological dependence to the possibility of accepting affective interdependence, forms part of the intentions of a psychoanalytic treatment regardless of the actual age of a patient. Furthermore, the age in years does not always guarantee psychological maturity.

Perhaps Diamond means to say that for adult men, or in old age, the sexual demand becomes less peremptory? According to my clinical experience, sometimes exactly the opposite is true. Some men of an advanced age, feeling that their sexual ability is at stake, can be even more exposed to the compulsive risk of regressing to phallic defences by entrusting their own identity and self-esteem to their possibility of performing the sexual act. (Our clinical practice is the privileged laboratory for our thinking, but I often wonder whether the increasingly frequent and distressing cases mentioned in the newspapers do not perhaps confirm this point).

It seems to me that the problem for many men is that it is difficult for them to keep at bay castration anxieties, the fear of annihilation, and their anxiety regarding impotence. In order to perform well, to feel certain of being able to have and maintain an erection, to penetrate, many men must sometimes resort to phallic defences or entrust, even though momentarily, the leadership in psycho-physical functioning to the phallic organisation.

Mature genital organisation—that is, full recognition of oneself and of the other in his or her entirety—is an ideal for men as it is for women, and each of us approaches it as best we can. Perhaps for a woman the problem, although equally as crucial, can be less obvious since she can easily dissimulate to herself and to her partner because she does not have to "show" or "demonstrate" anything at the concrete level about her ability to enjoy or give pleasure.

As for men, in my clinical experience, I increasingly ask myself whether the question is not so much men's fear of women (for example, the problem of impotence and of premature ejaculation can occur in hetero- as well as in homosexual relationships), but rather their fear of feeling whole in the relationship.

We could at this point wonder whether the difficulty of integration between the two different areas of tender exciting sensual contact and genital relationship is a problem that is specific to men. My point of view is that it concerns women and men equally; perhaps what changes is the type of defences used. But I am uncertain about this point because, for example, I have come across phallic defences in both women and men patients. (I am reminded of a very intelligent woman patient who was entrapped in an anobjectual imitative area and therefore with a reduced possibility of "seeing the other" and "being with someone". She had a strong phallic-narcissistic defence that was structured and carried out in her insistent and painful need to have power and control over everything, upheld by an omnipotent phantasy of superiority and impunity).

I would tend to hypothesise that perhaps it is the way in which a defence is organised and carried out that makes the difference. (Quite often, for example, in certain patients I have sometimes come across the tendency to defend themselves by resorting to a regressive area of illusion and ambiguity that disguised—at a different level—a defensive phallic quality).

In conclusion, we might ask ourselves whether the splendid "Song of Myself" by Walt Whitman, rather than describing a developmental conquest of wholeness, does not describe a return to an undifferentiated lost paradise, an area of illusion without time and without conflict.

References

Amati Mehler, J. (1992). Love and male impotence. *International Journal of Psycho-Analysis*, 73: 467–480.

Argentieri, S. (1985). Sulla cosiddetta disidentificazione dalla madre. *Rivista Psicoanalisi*, 31: 397–403.

Fajrajzen, S. (1973). Aspetti differenziali della simbiosi umana nei due sessio. *Rivista Psicoanalisi*, 19: 19–41.

Freud, S. (1900). *The Interpretation of Dreams. S. E., 4.* London: Hogarth.

Freud, S. (1912). On the universal tendency to debasement in the sphere of love. *S. E., 11*: 177–190. London: Hogarth.

Gaddini, E. (1968). Sulla imitazione. *Rivista Psicoanalisi*, 14: 235–260.

Gaddini, E. (1977). Formazione del padre e scena primaria. *Rivista Psicoanalisi*, 23: 157–183.

Greenson, R. R. (1968). Dis-identifying from mother: Its special importance for the boy. *International Journal of Psycho-Analysis*, 49: 370–374.

Pine, F. (1988). The four psychologies of psychoanalysis and their place in clinical work. *Journal of the American Psychoanalytic Association*, 36: 571–596.

Winnicott, D. W. (1956). On Transference. *International Journal of Psycho-Analysis*, 37: 386–388.

CHAPTER THREE

The hour of the stranger

James S. Rose

In thinking of "masculinity and femininity today" I have considered two questions: first, what do we understand by masculinity and femininity in current psychoanalytic terms, to what extent both characteristics are present in each individual, and how we can recognise these characteristics in patients of both sexes?; and second, taking into account "masculinity" and "femininity" as present in the analyst—male or female—how does this reflect in his/her analytic work and what limitations may be implied in the development of the "feminine" analytic function in a male, and vice versa?

I am going to try to respond to these questions by looking at how adolescents discover their sexuality and come to "own" their sexual bodies as they grow towards adulthood. One way of beginning to think about this is to propose that all adolescents encounter what D. H. Lawrence, in *Phantasia of the Unconscious*, called "the hour of the stranger". He took the view that there was a clear qualitative change in the adolescent and in their experience of themselves and others arising from the arrival of puberty. Thus:

> The child before puberty is quite another thing from the child after puberty. Strange indeed is this new birth, this rising from

35

the sea of childhood into a new being. It is a resurrection which
we fear .....

And now, a new world, a new heaven and a new earth. Now
new relationships are formed, the old ones must retire from their
prominence. Now mother and father inevitably give way before
masters and mistresses, brothers and sisters yield to friends. This
is the period of Schwarmerei (or excessive enthusiasm or sentimen-
tality), of young adoration and of real initial friendships. A child
before puberty has playmates.

After puberty he has friends and enemies.

It is the hour of the stranger. Let the stranger now enter the
soul.

And it is the first hour of true individuality, the first hour of
genuine, responsible solitariness. A child knows the abyss of for-
lornness. But an adolescent alone knows the strange pain of growing into his own isolation of individuality.

The strange pain of adolescents growing into their own isolation of
individuality was further explored by Winnicott. In one of his most
challenging papers, "Communicating and not communicating leading to a study of certain opposites" (1963), he explicitly examines this
process. It compresses into a few pages a number of ideas central to
his thought. I have found these ideas particularly relevant when thinking about the problems of treating adolescent patients and the special
difficulties that such an enterprise presents. Not least, this seems to
be concerned with the repeated discovery that some adolescents can
find the prospect of being helped by an adult almost subversive to the
development of their personality. As a result, they can strongly resist
treatment and give the psychoanalyst the feeling that they regard the
whole project as likely to lead to a grievous narcissistic injury. To my
mind, Winnicott captured this dilemma with the paradoxical proposal
that the adolescent must find a way to be isolated without having to be
insulated. This is a direct corollary of his idea that each individual is
an isolate, permanently non-communicating, permanently unknown,
in fact unfound.

We might say, therefore, that both Lawrence and Winnicott capture
something of the experience of what "adolescing" is about from the
point of view of both adolescents and their families. To go further into
this, I would like to discuss an eighteen-year-old adolescent, who came

for help expressing a feeling of a lack of confidence and fear when in the presence of other people. His lack of confidence expressed itself in his feeling that others looked down on him and, in particular, he was very anxious about what girls felt about him. He came at the recommendation of a teacher at the sixth form college he was attending. He had been living with his maternal grandmother for the past few years.

The significant facts that he reported of his family history were that his mother had suddenly left the family home when he was six; following which, he and his brother had lived with his father for a while. Their father then met and married his stepmother and they all tried to live together until the situation broke down because he found the new family unbearably trivial and superficial. As a result, he moved to his maternal grandmother's flat when he was eleven. This was experienced as very difficult, and consciously he had had little but contempt for his stepfamily. His therapy became very important to him and he experienced holiday breaks very keenly. It was clear that the strength of his feelings in the transference relationship made it possible for him to see the emotional link between what he perceived as other people's contempt for him and his own contempt for other people. He therefore communicated, by his enactments to me, the angry abandoning mother in his mind who, being always present in her absence, left him in a state of fear and helplessness. For example, at the beginning of treatment, he expected me to look down on his weakness for needing treatment. It took some time for him to be able to get in touch with his own contempt.

The significance of the facts about his life was, of course, not immediately obvious to him because it was the experience in which he lived. The difficulty he had in reflecting upon his experience meant that he expressed his difficulties by enactments in the transference. For example, at the end of sessions, he would look at me with an odd combination of fear and hatred and say "see you later" as he left with a slight air of contempt. The combination of these actions, in that moment, captured beautifully the one in his mind of his mother contemptuously leaving his father, with whom he identified. It seemed to me that it was an enactment in reverse, such that it represented exactly his feeling that I was dismissing him with contempt at the end of a session. This situation was then played out in his mind in his fantasies about girls. Thus, the manner of his mother's departure structured his mind, and its effect was revealed in the growing awareness of the experience of the end of each session.

As the meaning of this moment of separation became increasingly clear to us, it paved the way for him to find and visit his mother again for the first time in ten years, even though she lived not far away. Up to this point, his perception of his mother in his mind had been that she was harsh and rejecting. He discovered her not to be the heartless bully of his fantasies, but, actually, depressed. This was a profound shock to him because it upset all the fantasies he had built up to rationalise what had happened to him. He could now see that his fear of what girls thought about him arose from his unconscious hatred of women and, in particular, his mother. Hence, we could see that this unconscious hatred of women, implied by his conscious fear, had then been the stuff out of which the imagined hating mother had been created. His hatred had to be projected and denied because acknowledgement of it would mean having to assume responsibility for the departure of his loved object. The net effect of this psychic manoeuvre had been to void him of his aggression, which led, in turn, to his lack of confidence and the belief that others looked upon him with contempt. However, his lack of confidence was the price exacted for avoiding a conscious sense of his responsibility for his mother's departure. That is, his overriding but unconscious need to maintain his mother as a good object transformed the hatred of his loved mother into an unconscious belief, on his part, that his hatred of his mother had driven her away. The consequence of this belief being, and remaining, unconscious was that he was in consciousness afraid of her, as he was of all girls to whom he was attracted.

We could see how, in the re-encounter with his actual mother, the terrifying imagined mother was thrown into sharp relief and differentiated from his actual mother. This imagined mother had been created in the space left by the departure of his actual mother. It had then powerfully determined his psychic life and the conscious experience of his life. When he could see that this imagined figure was a product of his own mind, but had been experienced and perceived as if it were a fact of external reality, there was, after an initial profound shock, a considerable reduction in his anxiety. There was also a radical shift in his capacity to reflect on his own mind and a realisation that he did not necessarily know what was in the mind of the (m)other. The minds of others were there to be discovered and did not need to be automatically thought of as frightening or contemptuous.

Perhaps in confirmation of this hypothesis was the belief that developed in him that he needed to stay in contact with his mother to enable him to have a relationship with a girl. It was this that enabled him to replace the old hating mother with a present alive mother through whom he could create a relationship with a girl. The relationship with his mother went through many ups and downs. In any event, the gradual repair of this relationship enabled him to think of having a relationship with a girl, which he successfully achieved.

In this example, we can clearly see the impact on this young man's development of his parents' relationship and in particular upon his capability to develop a relationship with a girl. The fact that he felt that he needed to maintain his relationship with his mother in order to develop a relationship with a girl suggests that he had unconsciously believed that his difficulty in forming a relationship with a girl could be traced to his difficulties with his mother. Thus, girls had been strangers to him. Certainly, his rediscovery of his mother had been a strange experience for him and, as his belief in his rejecting mother crumbled, he gradually gained the confidence that he felt that he had lacked. This expressed itself not just in a new relationship but also with an increased occupational success. As he gained confidence in his abilities and skills, others recognised and appreciated the qualities of the emergent young man. Thus, I felt we could both see a wholly new sense of his bodily masculine identity; that is, what before was weak was now powerful and his sexual self was well able to enjoy, and be enjoyed by, a girl.

Gutton, with his notion of the pubertal, helps us to see something of the interaction between the arrival of the sexual body and the growing sense of an other with their own perspective, consciousness, and desires. "The pubertal" is an unfamiliar phrase coined to translate into English the French word "*pubertaire*", as distinct from "*puberté*", meaning puberty. In Gutton's (1991) view, the pubertal is to the psyche what puberty is to the body; or, the psychic consequences of the physiological changes brought about by puberty.

Gutton suggests that the meaning of these changes to the boy or the girl will not be confined to a changed body image or greater feelings of popularity and self-esteem but that there will be an experience of the newly potent genitalia in relation to (or, in fantasy, in the presence of) the genitalia of the opposite sex. Thus, he quotes Freud (1923) who says, "It is not until development has reached its completion at puberty that the sexual polarity coincides with male and female" (p. 145).

The psychic impact of what Gutton calls the pubertal is that puberty not only brings about a new conception of one's own body but also changes our conception of the body of the other sex and ushers in the idea of the complementarity of the sexes. This idea of the complementarity of the sexes creates a discontinuity in the sexual development of the individual because, for the first time, there is knowledge that the individual boy or girl can create a baby with a member of the other sex. Members of the two different camps can do something together; indeed, they complement one another. To my mind, this is what Freud (1905) meant when he said that sexuality becomes organised under the primacy of the genitals and that it becomes altruistic. Gutton (1991) continues: "Pubertal pressure has the aim of separating phallus and penis. Once the penis has been separated from its phallic significance, the female sex is revealed in the place where phallic castration had been expected".

Both sexes therefore have not only to incorporate the fact of their sexual bodies into their sense of themselves but also to incorporate the possibility of a new potential relationship between themselves and a member of the opposite sex. This is the consequence of complementarity. Perhaps it is this that is at the basis of the experience that something happens at, or around, puberty, which means that life, for the individual, will never be the same again. This very private experience ushers in a radical change in the developing adolescent's experience of his or her parents' relationship and of peers of the same sex and the opposite sex. All this is experienced within the matrix of the newly arrived sexual body. In essence, the pubertal represents the psychic meaning of the implication that the arrival of puberty has for the kind of relationships that the adolescent can expect to have with those of the opposite sex. This expectation will be based on that adolescent's observation of the parental relationship, whether the parents are physically present or absent in the adolescent's life.

This seems to point to the idea that the onset of adolescence, signified by puberty "turning up", represents a discontinuity in development, in that the individual experiences the possibility and prospect of something new and radically different in his or her life. To get a flavour of the implications of these dawning realisations for adolescents, let us look at Colette's novel *Le blé en herbe*, translated into English as *Green Wheat*.

Colette describes two adolescents—Phillipe and Vinca—sixteen and fifteen years respectively. They have known each other since childhood and each year their families have gone to the same place on the Brittany coast for their summer holidays. The novel is about the last few weeks of the summer holiday before their return to Paris with their parents.

Having grown up together we are told that "their entire childhoods bound them together, adolescence pulled them apart". One is aware, as a reader, of the gathering sense that this time the impending return to Paris will be different because the relationship between Phillipe and Vinca will have changed forever. Inseparable as children, fishing and swimming together throughout the endless holiday days of previous summers, there is a sense that these two have been seen by their parents as destined to marry and bring children of their own into the world. But the growing sense of the changes in their bodies and an awareness of their looks and appearance, seem portents of an entry into a new world of adulthood from which there is no turning away or avoidance. The summer holidays are, no doubt, a metaphor for adolescence and for the inevitability of it having to end and be followed by adulthood. What intrudes into Phillipe's gradually fading idyll is the arrival on the scene of Camille Dalleray—initially Madame Dalleray—who represents, and thus embodies, an adult sexual woman.

Throughout the novel, we get a sense of Phillipe's gradual anticipation of what the future holds for him: education and the baccalaureate; military service (this is France) and then a profession. He feels surrounded by the implicit parental expectation that he and Vinca will marry. We never really discover—and this is the power of the novel—whether these anticipations are entirely his own or are an edifice subtly built from his own desires intertwining with the desires of those around him. The main subjective focus of the novel is Phillipe but the reader is invited to observe him as he goes through a transition in his feelings about Vinca and, in particular, how he sees her.

To which, one must add, and how she sees him. Vinca, it is slowly revealed, is acutely aware of the changes going on within Phillipe. She also realises that something irreversible has occurred. As we see in the following passage, Vinca is no longer a child, any more than is Phil.

This passage begins with a reference to Phil believing that he has behaved in a less than worthy and rather infantile manner, not in keeping with what he sees as his approaching adulthood:

> "It doesn't? So you'll forgive me for acting like a little girl, so ridiculous?"
>
> She only hesitated a second: "Of course I'm going to forgive you, Phil. But even that won't change a thing".
>
> "About what?"
>
> "About us, Phil".
>
> She spoke with a sibylline softness that he didn't dare challenge further, and in which he didn't dare rejoice.
>
> Vinca no doubt followed the steps of his mental twists and turns, since she subtly added: "Do you remember the scenes you made, and the ones I made—it wasn't even three weeks ago—when we were so upset at having to cool off for four or five years before getting married? My poor Phil, I really wish I could turn the clock back and be a child again today".
>
> He waited for her to underline, to comment on that skilful, that insidious, "today" hanging in front of him in the pure and blue air of that August night. But Vinca already knew how to arm herself with silence.
>
> He insisted: "So, you're not holding it against me? Tomorrow we'll be … we'll be Vinca and Phil, the way we always were? Forever?"
>
> "Forever—if you want it, Phil … C'mon, let's go back inside. It's cold out here".
>
> She hadn't repeated, "the way we always were". But he contented himself with this incomplete vow and with the small, cold hand he held for a moment in his own. (1969, pp. 76–77)

Vinca recognises that, while their respective parents are felt to wish to unite them, she and Phillipe cannot be the way "they always were". In the text, this seems a private realisation. Knowing "how to arm herself with silence" is perhaps one of the most telling of the lines above, in that the choice of whether or not to communicate can feel like one of the new weapons acquired by the adolescent in her growing sense of individuality. However, this only feels like a weapon to those who relate to the adolescent, for they must live with the adolescent's right not to communicate as well as the new capacity to think. We see a new capacity to relate which, with the choice of whether to communicate or not, is evidence of the emergence of a new sense of self.

The silence of adolescents is perhaps one of the most troubling aspects of the experience of being their parents. There can seem to be an insurmountable wall between them, which can be puzzling and infuriating to both sides as they struggle with their incomprehension. For parents, few situations are as defeating as their desperation in response to the adolescent cry that "You don't understand me", when that is exactly what they are trying to do. Sometimes it stems from the adolescent— having just discovered a new sense of him or herself, which they find is a struggle to understand—refusing to have it be "understood" by well-meaning parents, because this will threaten, subtly, to undermine a very private achievement. It is so private that the adolescent is often only barely aware of it; but it makes possible a new kind of detachment that is able to withstand the pressure of strong feelings that can sweep away the capacity for what, to the adult world, is logical thought. As a result, it can often seem very difficult for adults to help or counsel adolescents because for those adolescents to accept help may well seem to threaten the growing sense of their maturity.

Now I want to focus on the notion of maturity. In discussing the adolescent position, Winnicott (1971) made the following observation.

> What I am writing here (dogmatically in order to be brief) is that the adolescent is immature. Immaturity is an essential element of health at adolescence. There is only one cure for immaturity and that is the passage of time and the growth into maturity that time may bring. Immaturity is a precious part of the adolescent scene. In this is contained the most exciting features of creative thought, new and fresh feeling, ideas for new living. Society needs to be shaken by the aspirations of those who are not responsible. If the adults abdicate, the adolescent becomes prematurely, and by false process, adult. (p. 146)

I think this passage is often taken as meaning that Winnicott felt that provided we give adolescents the freedom they apparently want, then all will eventually be well. But he says: "Advice to society could be: for the sake of adolescents, and of their immaturity, do not allow them to step up and attain a false maturity by handing over to them a responsibility that is not yet theirs, even though they may fight for it".

The clear implication is that adults must not confuse their perception of their adolescent children's irresponsibility with their own if they prematurely hand over a responsibility to them. We could say that the arrival of puberty puts into the hands of the adolescent a piece of equipment which they have to learn how to use. An adolescent girl, who seems to risk pregnancy carelessly, guards her fertility very carefully. She comes for a chlamydia test and, if infected, reports for treatment and brings her partner. From this it seems possible to suggest that the arrival of the sexual body has a much greater unconscious impact than is commonly assumed. We may wonder whether the awareness of the complementarity of the sexes means that adolescents look at their parents, and feel looked at by their parents, in a radically new way. Indeed, a stranger turns up with the arrival of puberty—both for the adolescent and for those around them.

Thus, when adolescents come for help from adults, it means that they are prepared to risk the consequence of encountering this stranger in themselves and in the other. This will not be in conscious awareness but will be expressed in their anxieties aroused by coming for help. Often they will say they find it difficult to talk about themselves. The desire to be silent reflects their wish to maintain a sense of themselves and their fear of this being subverted by opening themselves to other people. We might think that it reflects the features of the agoraphobic/claustrophobic shuttle. However, we are dealing here with a self in formation protecting itself from intrusion and not necessarily a dread of intimacy, as it might signify in an adult. We might say that they are in the process of coming to "know" themselves and do not wish this to be compromised by an adult apparently thinking they can know them before they can know themselves.

If we now return to the questions with which we began, we might review how what has been discussed above contributes to a response. The first question was: what do we understand by masculine and feminine, in current psychoanalytic terms, and to what extent are the characteristics of both present in each individual, and how can we recognise these characteristics in patients of both sexes?

Thinking about this first question, it seems to me that the case material above was an example of how the actual relationship between the adolescent's parents forms a set of assumptions about the relationship between a man and a woman which powerfully influence, and possibly determine, his expectations of girls. Thus, a mother/woman/wife rejects a father/man/husband with contempt and this structures this adolescent boy's perception both of himself and the other. Gutton's pubertal can, in this case, be seen as structuring this adolescent's conception of his own body as castrated and of a woman as being castrating. We also see that the sense of being masculine is intimately bound up with a sense of the feminine; and how the discovery of the reality of the mother as distinct from the internal representation enabled a discovery of the complementarity of the sexes—as opposed to a fundamental incompatibility. Thus, it is felt throughout the adolescent's being, in the sense of their awareness of their castrated body/self, which becomes confident and empowered, and in the relationship with the member of the other sex who changes from tyrant to comforting complementary being. We might therefore respond to the first question by saying that the important issue is not whether the characteristics of the genders are present in each individual but how both are represented and thus can be recognised.

This leads to the second question: taking into account "masculine" and "feminine" as present in the analyst—male or female—how is this reflected in his/her analytic work and what limitations may be implied in the development of the "feminine" analytic function in a male, and vice versa? I would like to respond by briefly discussing a case of a late adolescent girl on the brink of adulthood. At the outset, she described the same kind of lack of confidence and anxiety about boys as described in the case above. But, what was very apparent to me in my first meeting with her—we could say my countertransference—was how attractive and arousing she was to me, and yet she seemed to have no sense of her potential impact upon a male. To me she looked, in the vernacular, stunning, and was so from the first moment I met her. So apparent was this to me that I found myself wondering what colleagues would think of me if I described these countertransference feelings to them.

Her history made some sense of these feelings in that she said that she was the only child of a couple who had separated when she was eight years old. The cause of the separation was that her father had been discovered to have sexually abused her and was imprisoned. They were allowed to meet subsequently but only under strictly supervised conditions. Her mother, it was later revealed, had had an elder brother and they had been sexually inappropriate with each other in adolescence.

My patient's father appeared not to have been a sexually cruel predator but an ineffectual man who might well have been terrified of intimacy with an adult woman. As the work with this patient proceeded, it became clear that she found herself repeatedly getting involved with boys and becoming sexually engaged with them in a premature way. This culminated when she became involved in this way with a boy who had recently moved into the flat which she shared with others of both sexes. To her horror, after they had been sexually active with each other, she discovered that he was being sexually active with another girl who also lived in the same flat.

The brutality of this experience obviously had meaning for her as a developing young woman and as a child arrested in her sexual development by her father's abuse of her. It underlined her unconscious feelings of guilt for the incident with her father and how she sought to make masochistic reparation by becoming impulsively and prematurely sexually involved with young men who would treat her abusively. What was also apparent was her mother's inability to recognise her daughter as having any kind of emotional difficulty, for which I had some objective evidence quite apart from what my patient told me. As the work proceeded, it became clear that she needed a paternal figure to triangulate the experience of the abuse with the resultant experience of her father and the experience of her mother's apparent incognisance, which seemed to me to be possibly the result of an awful sense of guilt for having allowed the abuse to happen. In this case, it might well have been the result both of the abuse of her daughter by her husband and of what took place between herself and her brother.

In the treatment of this young woman, a complex transference emerged comprising an intertwining of the paternal/maternal and the masculine (penetrative)/feminine (containing). I felt I was being asked to contain powerful sexual feelings, thus enabling her to own her sexual feelings without the concomitant guilt repeatedly leading her into very painful re-experience of her abuse, which was destroying her capacity to engage in fruitful and rewarding relationships with male partners. It was noticeable that in the course of this treatment the power of my countertransference gradually receded, giving way to nurturing paternal feelings.

One might have expected this patient to have become phobic of her treatment because of an unconscious awareness of my transference/countertransference to her. But this did not seem to happen and she attended her sessions almost without exception. In one particular session, she described an incident which took place in the room in her flat where she had been sexually active with the former flatmate. She was with another male flat mate and became aware of how this young man was looking at her. She felt he was undressing her in his mind and became very self-conscious. She mentioned the name of the former flat mate, whom the young man knew, and knew what had happened. He replied by asking her why she had just mentioned his name. But this question seemed to be one to which they both knew the answer. She reflected that she had noticed that in many situations where a young man had shown a sexual interest in her, she had introduced something that would be unconsciously calculated to short-circuit where this interest might lead.

In the transference situation, it seemed to me that she was exploring what she saw going on between men and women with a father figure— her male psychoanalyst—who could help her understand young men's feelings and thereby help her to understand her own. At that moment, I chose not to draw her attention to what might be happening between us and confined myself to exploring her feelings about this young man for whom she felt much affection but was concerned that she might repeat the awful situation with the former flat mate. Given what I knew of her history with her father, it seemed crucial to be a containing father, fully experiencing the emotionally powerful oedipal situation while neither denying it to myself nor drawing attention to it directly.

I offer this clinical vignette as an example of the masculine and feminine as present in the analyst—in my case, male—to see how this was reflected in my analytic work. The limitations this implied in the development of the "feminine" analytic function in me, as a male, could not be confined to a containing function because I had to make it possible for us to think together about what had happened. In so far as analytic work involves holding the patient with one hand while performing surgery with the other, the most technically difficult aspect of the work involved addressing her complicity in her compulsive repetitions of the abuse because I felt this could easily arouse and reinforce her guilt. Yet this activity could not in my view be avoided. Potential for abuse by a persecuting superego thus emerged in the transference. However, through a slow working through of the incident with the flat-mate, she began to see what was driving her compulsion to repair the relationship with her father in order to regain the loved object she had brutally lost.

Concomitant with this compulsion was her lack of confidence in her capacity to develop a relationship with a male and her inability to protect herself from becoming prematurely sexually active. With this, of course, went her myopic stance to her attractiveness, possibly taking the form of an evacuative projection, which I vividly experienced in my countertransference. Thus, I think we again witness here the impact of the pubertal on the process leading this adolescent girl to a realisation of herself as an adult and sexual woman. By realisation, I do not confine myself to her becoming conscious of being a woman growing from having been a little girl. I also mean her realising her assets of being an adult woman capable of both attracting a young man, and of giving to him, appropriately and in a complementary manner.

In this case, what limitations this implied in the development of the "feminine" analytic function in a male seemed to me to be concerned with my avoiding any collusion with a phobia in me of being masculine/paternal. This phobia expressed itself to me in my fear of what my colleagues would think of me if I talked to them about my sexual feelings in the countertransference. So powerful were these feelings that it was hard for me to see them as countertransference (or my emotional response to the transference).

For some time, I felt they must be my own transference—arising from my own desire—and, for a while, they were somewhat disabling, or castrating. I wondered whether I had been somehow unconsciously introduced to the phantasies and experience of her abusing father. However, I think my function was to be a present containing father to enable this adolescent girl to explore her feelings about young men. In this way she could become a young woman in the fullest sense.

To return to the two questions with which we began: in response to the first, we might say that in understanding masculine and feminine, we have to take account of the impact of the arrival of the genital sexual body and the manner in which it acquires meaning in terms of the kinds of relationships that can be expected. Thus, there is no masculine without a feminine and vice versa. The sexual body's psychic meaning is partly determined by the adolescent's perception and experience of the parental relationship and the consequent identifications, be they with present or absent parental figures. The consequence is that both masculine and feminine must be present in each individual in some way. The only question is how this is structured. In the treatment of adolescents, the psychoanalyst's countertransference is a very important indication of how these identifications create intense difficulties for the young person concerned. Any dystonicity in the countertransference probably reflects what it is that the young person feels they must deny or avoid and may well feel quite counter-intuitive and/or conflictual to the treating psychoanalyst, as I found: for example, how can I feel like this and what will others think if I tell them?

In response to the second question, we might propose that there will be present in the treating psychoanalyst a pubertal structure embracing a conception of the relation between men and women. It will derive from the psychoanalyst's own experience of negotiating adolescence and will be modified by their personal analysis. It will provide a framework or matrix of experience to the negative hallucination of the relationship between the parental couple experienced in his own childhood. This then becomes the source of his dystonic feelings in the countertransference, of the kind identified above. It seems to me that this implies that the psychoanalyst of either sex—being an adult—will inevitably find his or her own pubertal structure disturbed when treating adolescents who are experiencing difficulties in negotiating this crucial stage in the sexual development leading them to adult identity. It is the adequacy with which the psychoanalyst's own pubertal has been analysed in his or her own personal analysis that sets the limitations in the development of the "feminine" analytic function in a male, and vice versa.

References

Colette, S. G. (1969). *Le blé en herbe*. Paris: Flammarion.

Freud, S. (1905). Three essays on the theory of sexuality. *S. E.*, 7: 123–246. London: Hogarth.

Freud, S. (1923). The infantile genital organization (An interpolation into the theory of sexuality). *S. E.*, 19: 139–146. London: Hogarth.

Gutton, P. (1991). *Le Pubertaire*. Paris: Presses Universitaires de France.

Lawrence, D. H. (1922). *Phantasia of the Unconscious*. New York: T Selzer.

Winnicott, D. W. (1963). Communicating and not communicating leading to a study of certain opposites. In: *The Maturational Processes and the Facilitating Environment: Studies in the Theory of Emotional Development*. London: The Hogarth Press and the Institute of Psycho-Analysis, 1965.

Winnicott, D. W. (1971). *Playing and Reality*. London: Tavistock Publications.

CHAPTER FOUR

Discussion of "The hour of the stranger"

Antònia Grimalt

The paper by James Rose is an interesting and complex paper which pushes our thinking in various directions. Rose explores the ways through which the adolescents discover their sexuality and, going deeper, he proposes two clinical vignettes. I will try to develop the ideas the paper has suggested to me, following the same order in which Rose explains his ideas.

My contribution will be centred on the recurrence of the infantile protomental in the adolescent. To do this, I will introduce the abstraction *container-contained* and I will speak of primary encapsulated nuclei that reappear in adolescence.

What we understand by masculine and feminine in current psychoanalytic terms

The first thing that occurred to me, when thinking about the issue of masculine and feminine in psychoanalytic terms, was Bion's model of the relationship *container-contained* ($\eth\,♀$) and the development by Tustin of infant bisexuality, in relationship with the primary integration of "soft" and "hard" sensations linked to pleasure and displeasure.

From a perspective of a personality with different coexisting levels separated/united by caesuras, the individual is at the same time structured/non structured, differentiated/fused, assertive/receptive. All of this determines the dialectics reflected in the dilemma of how to reconcile the need to be assertive and at the same time be able to relate or to affirm one's own desire while recognising that of the other. This dilemma emerges intensely in adolescence when there is an activation of the preoedipal determinants of a gender identity, linked to separation and differentiation. The strangeness and lack of connection pervade the adolescent experiences, as Rose suggests in the title of his paper: The hour of the stranger. An unknown experience where body/mind, sexuality/identity, sexual differences/individual construction, and fusion/differentiation undergo changes and acquire new dimensions. The developmental crisis represents a new opportunity for the integration of these elements.

Bion (1962) raises the abstraction *container-contained* as a complex link which goes from the most elemental and primary sensory-emotional relationship to the most complex thought developments. He represents this relationship, where the two partners have an active part with reciprocal mutuality, by the signs *masculine-feminine* ($\male\female$). Every object of the relationship embodies multiple possibilities of sameness and difference, masculinity and femininity. The mother's "reverie" in her process of containment transforms the catastrophic experience of helplessness into a bearable emotion, and furnishes the elements to process emotions and to modulate pain. There is a tendency to surround the function of *container-receptive* by an idealised halo of passivity. However, the containment and processing of ambivalent feelings in the relationship with the baby (and, at another level, of the analyst in relationship to the patient), to offer a space for the otherness, are not passive at all. I think Rose conveys this process eloquently in the second case. In the analytic situation the patient and analyst must relinquish the idealisation of the container function and the narcissistic satisfaction respectively, so as not to end in a parasitic atemporal relationship.

Psychic bisexuality can be understood as a self quality, in relationship to the masculine and feminine, as pure elements which show the double primary orientation to the object: *to be the object* which implies primary identification with it and to *have the object* which implies differentiation and from it the drive activity (Ferraro, 2003). This second meaning keeps a more explicit anchorage with the sexual gender and with the parental couple and implies a double parental identification, maternal and paternal.

The mother's attitude and her capacity to allow her child to go from a dyadic relationship to the triadic one with the father and herself, must have a correspondence in the container function, by the father, of the mother-baby relationship. The developmental child perceives not only the representation which he has in the father's mind but, specially, the representation the father has of the child-in-relationship-with-the mother (Fonagy & Target, 1995; Target & Fonagy, 2002). From then on, there is a development of a second level representation which promotes the abstract thinking. This process (maternal-paternal) is rooted again in the parent's memories and mental images of the triadic relationships with their own parents and in their understanding of the difference between generations. The container-contained relationship ($\male\female$) sets up *masculine* and *feminine* as containing each other and feeding the personal evolution of the couple and their children.

Tustin (1981) conceives the infant bisexuality as the primary integration between "hard" (penetrating) and "soft" (receptive) associated initially to pleasure and displeasure. The primary undifferentiation state, in its dialectics of union and duality explosions, needs to be contained. When things go smoothly, mother and baby attune rhythms, facial expressions, vocalisations, or actions. The imitation develops into a process of introjective identification as a reciprocal and complementary relationship, rather than competitive and parasitic. If a failure in the attunement occurs, the infant experiences a premature loss of the primary oneness and feels thrown into a premature duality. At this level, the pain induced by the absence of satisfaction can be felt as a void; the painful emotion is neither registered nor processed, and in its place there is an emotional void, an area of *"non existence"* (Bion, 1962), which remains as a hole in the experience of the self.

The non-processed emotional experiences remain as *non-mentalised facts*, neither conscious nor unconscious but unreachable because of the lack of transformational systems which would allow their observation and comprehension: they belong to an archaic functioning that goes through the time caesura between the pre-conceptual primitive and the verbal actual. These gaps and voids in the emotional processing lead to a search for sensation and action as a survival manoeuvre, to diminish the lived anxieties, in resonance with non-mentalised facts of the primary infancy.

The obstacles in the primary development can render difficult the normal developmental splitting (linked to the register and processing of emotion) which the infant needs in order to maintain a creative relationship with the other. Instead of this, there can appear a false splitting at the level of gender difference where the "bad" is found on one side of the sexual and the "ideal" on the other side. It appears as a failure in the integration of the bisexual desires in relationship to both parents. It manifests itself, for example, in homosexuality where there is a phobic avoiding of the opposite sex and an unbridled race to catch the (idealised) object of the same sex (McDougall, 1978).

The adolescent's discovery of sexuality and the process of mentalisation of his/her body

In Rose's experiential description of the adolescent, he speaks about the qualitative change of his or her own self experience and the experience of others: the strangeness of a new birth, an emergence from the childhood sea in a new beginning. The otherness, essential to promote the encounter with the other, is born from the primary relationship: from the mother's capacity to attune with the desires for autonomy, together with the child's own capacity to differentiate. The child who has not been able to feel the psychic security needed to differentiate himself from his primary object will remain immersed in a world ruled by the other's affective processes. I think something similar happens, in different ways, in both clinical cases presented.

Winnicott, in his 1963 paper, describes the primitive *subjective* (non differentiated) perception and the evolution to the *objective* perception (quoted in Kumin, 1996). When the child is capable of perceiving the object in an *objective* way (to the pre-objectal relationship is added the objectal one), he becomes able to communicate and not communicate. However, there are adolescent ways of phantasising, very near to sensoriality, where this level of no communication is used to recreate a lost fusional state and not a creative process of differentiation.

I agree with the idea that the arrival of the adolescent body has an unconscious impact greater than is normally supposed. The pubertal emerges from a genital experience which has to do with the sensorial. The metamorphosis that it brings is so deep that Gutton (2005) adopts the term of "pubertal archaic" because he thinks that the mechanisms of functioning are very similar to the baby's, only that it is now a matter of a genital theme. The childhood attachments change and the force of the new experiences of the second phase of sexuality reorganises them.

The sensoriality outburst in the adolescent reverberates the sensorial invasion that the foetus undergoes when changing from the protected world in the uterus to the invading chaos of unknown stimulae of the external world. The reverberation of early experiences, at another level of the spiral, implies the challenge of coming to "own" his/her sexual body, in a growing body, and his/her own sexual awakenings, as Rose illustrates. At the beginning of life, the mind starts functioning, trying to process the body bio-vital drives, providing them with a direction. In adolescence, the mind is invaded by the body changes, this time non-undifferentiated, like the baby's, but endowed with a specific *corporeity*, masculine or feminine (Ferrari, 2004). The adolescent becomes a *body*, in other words, "it takes over a *corporeal shape*" which needs emotional processing and implies intense pain: he/she must deal with a body that does not belong to him/her anymore. The overburdening external and internal physical and psychological changes provoke the reactivation of survival manoeuvres centred in the body and ruled by the sensoriality. I agree that some disharmonious behaviour in the adolescent is not always related to pathology but rather to the process of learning by experience.

If the process of emotional development is partially halted, the adolescent feels pushed to use his/her own sensations to lessen unconsciously felt anxieties, which echo non mentalised facts of early childhood. The psychoanalytic relationship can be crucial to redress the mental and emotional growing. The silent aspects of the setting, with its characteristics of rhythm, consistency, and regularity (which evoke the early basic rhythm), can establish an essential basis for the transformation and emotional processing in a new relational experience. However, this is not an easy task because the adolescent feels that nobody understands him/her, which is true, because nobody has had his/her specific and personal experiences. When somebody approaches him/her (as Rose comments) he/she immediately feels disturbed and, sometimes, as if it were a matter of being robbed of his/her experience. It can be said that, paradoxically, *incommunicability* is the adolescent's first form of *communication*.

The sensorial and affective burden awakens early anxieties in the claustro-agoraphobic register. I think that the panic of feeling trapped inside the object provokes this new distance from the parents' world (or from the therapist), as Rose suggests. At the same time, he/she experiences the terror to fall back on the void. How to find the way to be alone without feeling lost in the nothingness? Or, as Rose points out, how to be isolated without having to be insulated, being *confined*? How to contain these strong sensations and emotions without enough psychic structure to contain them? On one side the terror of the void, and on the other side the panic of being lost inside the other.

A concrete presence of an absence

Rose introduces us to an eighteen-year-old adolescent, who comes to the consultation on a teacher's recommendation. The patient describes a sensation of insecurity and fear in relationships, out of a feeling of being despised, which is more intense with girls. I will comment on the hypothesis and questions this suggested to me.

It seems that the central nucleus of the patient's construction of his history (and it appears structured in his mind as a link self-object, distant, rejecting, and abandoning) is one where the mother, *suddenly*, left the father when the patient was six. Rose conveys the patient's lack of affective reflective resonance faced with such a relevant fact. In Rose's own words: "the importance of his own history was not immediately evident to him, and the difficulty in reflecting on it drove him to show his problems through enactments in the transference". When it does not evoke any memories of his own (as if there had never been any inscription in a void area in his mind), this suggests non-processed, frozen emotions which remained hijacked and evacuated in a static image of rejection. The patient seemed neither to have a mind of his own, nor to be conscious of the difficulty in processing his emotions. He said that the problem was his parents' separation, not the loss of his mother: as if everything would happen in the other's mind. All in all, it suggests a gap between a primary affectivity representation, on the one side, and the oedipal representations, on the other: a group of non-mentalised emotions not articulated with the representation.

Continuing with the history: the father meets and marries the patient's stepmother. Could we conjecture that there was a breaking of an unconscious fusional link with the father which gave way to a feeling of futility and loss of meaning faced with an experience which he felt to be a new rejection and abandonment? We do not know about his relationship with his brother. At the age of eleven he goes to live with his grandmother and we are told that this is a difficult process. Could it mean trying to escape from a void to look for affection and meaning with another relationship?

We are told that, at the beginning, he transfers to the analyst a cold and distant object who rejects and despises any need, felt as a manifestation of weakness. There then appeared strong feelings in the transference relationship, which permitted the observation of the enactment of a link self-object that was cold, distant, and rejecting, experienced alternately by both members of the therapeutic couple. I wonder about the atmosphere during the session and the strong feelings which were given expression in a nonverbal way at the moment of separation: what kind of contratransferential feelings could he provoke? A hypothesis of an alienating identification non-represented with a distant and cold object suggests contratransferential feelings of void, futility, and a lack of meaning. Perhaps Rose could intuit that, under all of this, there was a strong demand that was disheartened and despairing? How can a non-represented absent object be transferred, if not as absenting himself affectively? If it was like this, then it was probably not easy to make sense of this entire situation.

I have the impression that the kind of anxiety felt when leaving, was not due to separation from a represented object, but rather to the sudden disappearance of a part of the self fused with the object, with the consequent feeling of void. The combination of fear and hatred, when leaving, could be the expression of an intense emotion, non symbolized, due to the difficulty of processing the loss, deprivation, coldness and aloneness. This silent affective reaction, which Rose is able to observe, suggests an experience of imperceptible terror linked to an encapsulated nucleus of primitive experience. Could it mean a lot of early microtraumatic states which, as a condensation of repeated experiences of affective abandonment, took shape in the image of the mother *suddenly* abandoning the father? The word "suddenly" suggests an unforeseeable feeling of remaining suspended in the void without any place on which to hang.

The regularity and consistency of time and space of the setting, together with a firm and containing attitude based on an empathic understanding, probably created a mental atmosphere, emotional and physical, which furnished a basic rhythm where there could emerge meaning for the mute areas and non-processed emotions. My hypothesis is that the analyst recreated the parental communication in his oneiric-affective space, as a true gestation of the patient's potential self, being able to observe, contain, and name a series of non-mentalised emotions. The patient's process of becoming conscious of his mind being different to the object's mind, together with the capacity to become conscious of his own anger, created the basis of a triangular space with the possibility of reflective thinking. It is evident that the patient unconsciously knew that the basis of his difficulties in establishing a love relationship started in his difficulties in the relationship with the mother.

An invading presence

In the second clinical vignette, we are told about similar symptoms of anxiety and insecurity in relationships with the opposite sex in a young woman sexually abused by his father when she was eight years old, and the subsequent separation of her parents. At the same time, there is something that suggests a possible enigmatic transgenerational message through the mother and her lack of emotional contact with her daughter's emotions. All in all, it suggests the existence of difficulties in the emotional processing and subjective ownership of her experiences. We have in this case an invading presence which disturbs the patient's sexual development.

In his case description, the analyst eloquently shows the massive sensorial invasion in his mind which gives way to shame and *guilt*. His containing function is then disturbed and it takes time for him to distance himself in order to transform the emotions and abstract a meaning from a "third position" (Britton, 1998).

In the analytic relationship there is an enactment of a non-contained sensoriality not transformed into affection through the relationship. I totally agree with the idea that the patient unconsciously reproduced her phantasies and unbearable experiences stirred up by an abusing father. It seems that the experience of abuse, together with her mother's lack of emotional resonance (because of a negation of her guilt?), drives the patient to engage in sexual relationships in a premature and compulsive way, as if her desire for emotional contact and understanding were confused with the psychic fusional contact.

The analyst conveys his vivid consciousness of his patient's need not to feel trapped in his desire, to be able to develop her own desire and to find her own voice, and, from that, his brilliant description of the intertwining of the paternal/maternal and the masculine (penetrative)/

feminine (containing). In his own words: "to contain powerful sexual feelings thus enabling her to own her sexual feelings without the concomitant guilt repeatedly leading her into very painful re-experience of her abuse which was destroying her capacity to engage in fruitful and rewarding relationships with male partners". At the same time, he raises the issue of how, at some moments, the direct transference interpretation could be felt by the patient as an invasion and abuse by a persecutory superego. So he describes the need to be a present containing father who fully experiences the oedipal situation, neither denying it nor trying to call direct attention to it. However, he also brings up the issue that the containing and transforming of his own emotions is not enough, and it is necessary to look for the words to open the process of thinking together.

> How "masculine" and "feminine" reflect in the analytic work and what limitations this may imply in the development of the "feminine" analytic function or a "masculine" analytic function depending on the analyst being a man or a woman.

I do agree that masculine does not exist without feminine. The problem, as Rose points out, is how this presence is structured. If things go well, it will structure itself as an internalised link in a creative and complementary dynamic interaction.

I consider the psychic bisexuality as closely linked to differentiation; the concrete bisexuality represents the rejection of sexual differences and the recognition of the lack of the other sex. The emotional disturbance is a consequence of a splitting between the feminine and masculine elements of the personality: one part does not contain the other and vice versa; the container-contained relationship is negative. If this splitting is not solved, the person looks for a sensorial relationship without affective implication or the looking for it becomes inhibited.

If we leave aside the gender conception, and we focus on the concept of function, the analyst necessarily integrates both aspects in a binocular perspective, as a capacity to take in the verbal and nonverbal communication. He needs to register and process his/her own emotions, to contain them; to transform his/her own countertransference and counterprojective identification, and to be able to return to the reality of the relationship: the feminine function in his/her capacity to observe, to give space, and to contain, and the masculine function in the capacity to distance oneself from the patient's most immediate projections and to offer a different perspective from a "third position" (Britton, 1998). As analysts, we are always dramatising one or other aspect of the oedipal dynamic. The function of a third helps us to "objectivise", to distance ourselves from the most immediate projections, and to offer the patient a different perspective. However, it is not always easy to elucidate the kind of projection that the patient does; detecting it is sometimes complicated by the difficulty we find in ourselves to feel reflected in the image that the patient projects in us. Sometimes we need a "second opinion" to be able to get out of the collusion.

In the adolescent, the impact of the arrival of the sexual genital body needs an intense process of metabolization and search for meaning. I agree with the fact that the body's sexual psychic meaning is determined by the adolescent's perception and experience of the parental relationship and his/her identifications with both parents. However, I would add that all of this is closely linked with the psychic meaning conferred by parents. This meaning, as I said before, is based, in turn, on the parents' memories and mental images of the triadic relationships with their own parents and their understanding of the generational difference. The same happens, at an analogous level, in the analytic relationship.

It is in this way that I understand the author's final comments, when he says that the pubertal structure of the analyst will inevitably be disturbed when treating patients who experience difficulties in this process. The analyst has his/her own conception of the relationship between men and women, which stems from his/her own pubertal experience, modified by the personal analysis. Rose states that it will provide a framework or matrix of experience to the negative hallucination of the relationship between the parental couple experienced in their own childhood. From there dystonic feelings in the countertransference can then emerge as he describes in the second case. The capacity to register these conflictive feelings, which represent an obstacle for the intuition, allows Rose to sense complicated identifications which the young person feels he/she must deny or avoid.

References

Bion, W. R. (1962). *Learning from Experience*. London: Heimann.
Britton, R. (1998). Subjectivity, objectivity and triangular space. In: *Belief and Imagination*. London. Routledge.

Diamond, M. J. (2004). Accessing the multitude within: A psychoanalytic perspective on the transformation of masculinity at mid-life. *International Journal of Psycho-Analysis*, 85: 45–64.

Diamond, M. J. (2009). Masculinity and its discontents: Making room for the "mother" inside the male—an essential achievement for healthy-male gender identity. In: B. Reis & R. Grossmark (Eds.), *Heterosexual Masculinities. Contemporary Perspectives from Psychoanalytic Gender Theory* (pp. 23–54). New York & Hove, E. Sussex: Routledge.

Ferrari, A. B. (2004). *From the Eclipse of the Body to the Dawn of Thought*. London: Free Association Books.

Ferraro, F. (2003). Psychic bisexuality and creativity. *International Journal of Psycho-Analysis*, 84: 1451–1467.

Fonagy, P. & Target, M. (1995). Towards understanding violence: the use of the body and the rôle of the father. *International Journal of Psycho-Analysis*, 76: 487–502.

Grimalt, A. (2007). Reversing perspective: Time<–>Timelessness. *European Psychoanalytic Federation Bulletin*, 65.

Gutton, P. H. (2005). *Adolescence et memoire*. Service de Psychiatrie et de Psychologie Medicale CHU Angers. http://www.med.univ-angers.fr/discipline/pedopsy/Publications/gutton2005.htm

Kumin, I. (1996). *Pre-object Relatedness: Early Attachment and the Psychoanalytic Situation*. New York: The Gilford Press.

McDougall, J. (1978). *Plaidoyer pour une certaine anormalité*. Paris: Ed. Gallimard.

Target, M. & Fonagy, P. (2002). Fathers in modern psychoanalysis and in society: the role of the father and child development. In: Trowell, J. & Etchegoyen, A. (Eds.), *The Importance of Fathers*. London: The New Library of Psychoanalysis.

Torras, E. (1987). A contribution to the papers on transference by Eva Lester and Marianne Goldberger & Dorothy Evans. *International Journal of Psycho-Analysis*, 68: 63–67.

Tustin, F. (1981). Psychological birth and psychological catastrophe. In: J. S. Grotstein (Ed.), *Do I Dare Disturb the Universe?* London: Karnac.

CHAPTER FIVE

The abyss of intimacy

Jacqueline Amati Mehler

For decades, feminine sexuality has been considered the obscure area of psychoanalytic theorisations, as though everything regarding masculine sexuality had, instead, been totally clarified. Is this really true? Some authors have claimed that masculine sexuality is the same as it was fifty years ago; what has changed is the social condition of women. However, changes in the social condition of women, and their impact on the relations between men and women, have altered many certainties; furthermore, changes within the more general aspects of sexuality have occurred.

While a lot has been written about women's subordination and exploitation, and about women's sexual liberation, only very few authors (sociologists, journalists, but almost no analysts) have attempted to explore the intimate and deep changes that the sexual liberation of women has brought about in the relationship between men and women.

Most of these publications have a psycho-social ideological approach to debating whether males and females are alike or whether they are different and, in this case, to the discussion of the main differences. Some more sophisticated writers have analysed the image of one or the other gender in myths and different cultures and give a phenomenological description of current changes in the male-female relationship.

Nevertheless, publications about manhood predicted, as an outcome of a self-examining conscience, a "new male" at the "time of fallen heroes".

I will not dwell here on the controversial debate about whether women have really achieved autonomy and sexual liberation, or whether men have really changed their behaviour towards women over the last decade. Certainly, this controversy could be contextualised within more precise data regarding different cultures or age groups and the result of such research could eventually modify the perspective of some of my own assumptions. However, my present discussion is merely based on clinical observations derived from my experience with male and female patients over the last several years.

Over the last decades the vicissitudes of intimacy have claimed our psychoanalytic attention from a deeper perspective, owing to our increased knowledge of the more primitive areas of psychic functioning. Issues of nature (anatomy, neurology, genetics, hormones, etc) versus culture are, of course, at the centre of more "scientific" argumentations but the shared view is that something different is inhabiting the field of male-female intimate interactions. It is this aspect that has intruded into my clinical understanding of some of the classical sexual problems that we encounter in our patients. Among these, chance led me to pay particular attention to the problems of male sexuality, especially male impotence, because I encountered this problem more frequently than in the earlier days of my clinical practice. I became particularly interested in its relation to love and to object relations and I was struck by how little literature there was on this subject.

I have discussed elsewhere (1992), with abundant clinical material, the question of male impotence in relation to the issue of separation-individuation as it displays itself in the transference-countertransference interaction. Whereas my attention had primarily focused, in individual cases, on the relation between the vicissitudes of the early phase of symbiotic undifferentiation and its connection with the clinical manifestation of impotence within a heterosexual love relation, I have lately started to wonder about the impact of the current generalised social and cultural tendency towards sexual undifferentiation on the fate of individual identity, its role in child development and in interpersonal heterosexual relations.

During the years in which transformations in sexual habits were developing, "unisex"—if I may use a more or less wild analogy— seemed to have become equivalent to *"egalité, liberté, fraternité"*. I think that a dramatic confusion has taken place between socio-ideological levels on one hand, and psychological levels on the other. To those who claim that men and women differ very little at the level of psychosexual development, I would like to recall another famous French phrase (albeit rejecting its original discriminatory meaning!) that says: "*Vive la petite différence*"! The gay anti-discrimination campaign promoted sociocultural changes leading to the recognition by the European Community of homosexual marriage and the recommendation that these couples be granted the right to adopt children. Biotechnological developments confront us with virginal women who—like the Madonna—become mothers without having ever had a sexual relation, and with grandmothers who become biological mothers of their own grandchildren procreated with the son-in-law's seed. Thus, many natural boundaries that were considered unsurmountable, such as gender or generational frontiers, are being progressively overcome by science and by habits.

This step deserves thorough discussion in all its complex human, legal, and sociological aspects, but this would require yet another paper. I would only like to call attention now to what appears to me to be an irreversible, slow undifferentiating trend that might—at least partly—derive from a misunderstanding of psychological tenets in relation to family interactions and to child rearing practices. Nobody nowadays would object to men sharing what used to once be only "feminine tasks", or to fathers sharing child care. We have also become more subtle in distinguishing in our analyses between father and mother as male and female, and "paternal" and "maternal" as being interchangeable functions regardless of the gender. However, I cannot help wondering about further steps taken in the direction of total confusion between mother and father, and to illustrate my point I shall describe an example that I was able to observe personally, several years ago, of "advanced" child care counselling in the feeding of newborn babies.

In special cases of mothers who initially do not have enough milk to feed their babies, and/or of babies who do not suck sufficiently, the extra milk pumped from the mother's breasts in-between feedings is put into a special bottle that has two thin tubes coming out of the lid from which the milk can flow. During breast feeding, the mother tapes the tubes to her nipples so that the baby sucks from both nipple and the tubes, thus achieving stimulation of the breast milk as well as reducing the child's frustration. When the mother is resting or working and the father feeds the baby, rather than using a plain feeding bottle with a teat, he does so with this same special bottle containing the milk pumped from the mother's breast. In order to provide the baby with an experience as close as possible to having mother's nipple in the mouth, father is advised to tape the two tubes to his finger and to then introduce it into the baby's mouth, who sucks the finger together with the milk flowing from the tubes. (I shall abstain from confessing my own perverse phantasies when I saw this.) We could ask, of course, what is to prevent the further step of father taping the tubes to his own nipple, in the same way as the mother! Besides consequences to the child's capacity to differentiate father from mother, and him or herself from the two different primary objects (about which we can only speculate), I think we could wonder about such medical advice and its connection to man's deep unconscious envy of maternal functions disguised under shared parenthood responsibilities.

Let me return to the point from which my reflections started, namely to the attempt to understand the underlying vicissitudes of male sexuality. Most literature dealing with masculine impotence views this disturbance in relation to castration anxiety, or like Klein (1946) and her followers, to early anxieties connected with phantasies of "attacking and sadistically entering the mother's body" which would also contain father's penis, and lead to the dread of mother herself.

Although classical Freudian formulations relating impotence to the fixation to incestuous phantasies retain all their validity, two questions require further attention in my mind. First, I think that there are many different forms of impotence: we are dealing with a symptom rather than with a specific psychopathological entity. Secondly, I believe that what has not been sufficiently attended to is the contribution that knowledge about earlier processes of psychic organization and development—in which the self and the object are fused and undifferentiated—can lead to a better understanding of sexual impotence.

In "A special type of choice of object made by men" Freud (1910) describes ways in which neurotic men behave in love: enacting the tendency to make an engaged woman the object of their love and thus gratifying impulses of rivalry and hostility connected with the oedipal situation; experiencing conscious and unconscious conflict between the choice of either an idealised and highly valued woman, or of a debased prostitute-like surrogate of the "instinctual" mother. In "On the universal tendency to debasement in the sphere of love", Freud (1912) gives perhaps his most explicit contribution to the understanding of masculine impotence, claiming that:

> ... foundation of the disorder is provided by an inhibition in the developmental history of the libido before it assumes the form which we take to be its normal termination ... An incestuous fixation ... plays a predominant part in this pathogenic material and is its most universal content ... Two currents, whose union is necessary to ensure a completely normal attitude in love have, in the cases we are considering, failed to combine. These two may be distinguished as the affectionate and the sensual current. (p. 180)

When affection and sensuality are not linked but are opposed, due to fixation to incestuous phantasies, the capacity to love will be marked by this split. "Restriction has thus been placed on object choice" (Freud, 1910). The affectionate sensual current and the sexual wish can only seek gratification from two different objects since fusion of both currents has failed. Longstanding social conventions that considered it normal for a man to have extramarital affairs allowed—with minimum conflict—for this internal scenario to be syntonic with external reality. Moreover, a widespread conception of manhood, confirmed through permanent conquest of sexual objects, allowed for the reinforcement of defensive splitting of object choice.

While Freud uses the terms "sexual" and "sensual" as synonyms, I think it is important to differentiate these two components in order to deepen our understanding of love and its vicissitudes, impotence, and, probably, frigidity as well. Freud does not take into consideration early partial objects; he refers to the object as a target of drive investment in relation to the developmental phases (oral, anal, and phallic) that converge in the genital organisation with the resolution of the oedipal conflict.

However, differently from Klein for whom the object, although partial, exists since the beginning, the Freudian theorisations about drive vicissitudes suggest that the psychoanalytic object will be construed to the extent that the sexual drive will be anaclitically linked to the nurturing self-preservative function. In other words the pre-objectual phase is bound to needs whereas, successively, wishes and conflict will organise themselves following investment in the object gradually conceived as being relatively separate from the self. From this viewpoint, when Freud mentions the affectionate current, he refers to more or less sublimated or de-sexualised libido. Other authors, such as Gaddini, consider in the place of the temporal developmental phases, areas of development or different functional levels—a psycho-sensorial area related to sensations and a psycho-oral area related to drives and conflict. The latter, it is implied, formulate the coexistence of different experiential levels even in more developed adults.

Such conceptualisations allow us to further clarify the difference between sensuality and sexuality. *Sensuality* as I am viewing it here is connected with pleasure provided by sense organs which, starting in the infant from undifferentiated auto-sensual-eroticism, moves via transitional activities towards the integration of sensations within the self-object dialogical vicissitudes. (According to those who follow Winnicott and Mahler, drives are not discarded but, differently from Freud, they do not address (invest) the object that will only take its shape and place following individuation and separation processes). *Sexuality* in its more mature, genital expressions includes sensuality as the earliest phases of "affection", but entails the emergence of object-directed libidinal and aggressive drives. When I refer to mature genital love I also do not refer solely to the Freudian concept of a genital libidinal level of partial drives, but also to the degree of self-object differentiation processes which, according to clinical experience, do not always run along parallel lines. I realise that none of these models account in a satisfactory way for the combined and parallel development of drives, nor of gender identity formation and the discrepancies between the self, the subject, and the object. This is even more complex if we consider those theorisations that instead of referring to the temporal developmental phases, invoke coexisting levels (to which I also refer) whereby within a well-developed psychological organisation there exist oscillations between fusional and genital levels of functioning.

What has been neglected, in my mind, is that what may be impossible to integrate within the same relation is not only affection and sexuality, as described by Freud, but also—and perhaps even primarily—the merging of fusional and genital levels of experience, both being intrinsic and essential parts of love and intercourse; what appears to be extremely threatening regards the implied degree of regression at various levels for such experiences to co-exist. Here I make a distinction between a tender affection carrying a sensual stream, linked to regressive fusional experience, and a different kind of affection which does not prevalently involve such merging experiences. The first one, marked by early concrete bodily experiences, can be resumed in all its infantile polymorphism (albeit fused with genitality) in the service of love and mature sexuality.

It thus follows that I am referring to two different kinds of vicissitudes within the "coexistence" of affection and sexuality. One regards the object choice (idealised or debased, according to Freud) bearing on and manifesting itself along *interpersonal* lines. The other regards the *intrapsychic* capacity to bear regression and deliver oneself with the same object in shared passion and genital love, to the most primary erotic affection, embedded in the "oceanic" totalising symbiotic experience that lacks boundaries between self and object. Disturbances of either kind of "co-existence" of affection and sexuality—whether regarding object choice or the capacity for deep intimate closeness with the object, at different levels—can be variably organised in normal life and in neurosis, confronting us with varying and compound conditions of impotence (or frigidity?), according to the eventual admixture with other neurotic components.

In some cases we are dealing with total impotence due to lack or inhibition of desire. For such men this condition is independent of a real available object and depends on their own faithful libidinal allegiance to the unconscious incestuous (prohibited) object.

In other cases we find a selective impotence, so well described by Freud when dealing with the case of men who, impotent with an idealised mother figure, can have "normal" intercourse with devaluated debased "instinctual like" mother surrogates. Sometimes these men may run into total frightening impotence when they are sexually involved with a partner who, appearing initially as a superficial affair, is liable to become more than the object of a split sexual investment. The temporary fall of defences renders the liaison a threatening source of haunting, infantile, incestuous phantasies. A compromise situation may be set up, whereby a partial debasement of the object (considered "just" a sexual object) and a constant phobic-like attitude, maintaining the object neither too close nor too detached, can represent an attempt to grant survival to such a relationship if it meets the object's implicit collusion.

Among those particular instances that account for intermittent or occasional impotence—increasingly frequent in our practice—we come across men who have hitherto functioned well when engaging in more or less free, affectionate, or stable relations, but who, upon falling deeply in love, are unable to have intercourse with their new partner and react with intense anxiety and despair to such a paradoxical situation. It is precisely the perception of a major involvement, more intense or "different" from previous ones, that is frightening and felt as a threat to their usual internal set up and stability.

Other men can function well sexually with their life partner—who may often be frigid or unresponsive—while they run into incipient states of transitory impotence if involved with sexually responsive partners. As mentioned above, the crisis of impotence coincides with the highest peak of desire and simultaneous defence from closeness. (Other forms of impotence manifest themselves through premature ejaculation or protracted erection with anorgasmia).

I think that cases of covert potential impotence are more frequently uncovered today by virtue of the changes in social and sexual habits following women's emancipation. More freedom, and decrease of sexual inhibition, have implications both in the cases of men who tend to make split object choices and in those who fear intimacy and merging experiences with the object. As I noted before, in the traditional set-up (when separation and divorce were unusual), it was natural and standard for men to conduct multiple sexual relations (while remaining attached to a non-sexualized mother-like central figure). This enhanced and allowed for a "physiological" split of object-roles as described by Freud. While this is still an ongoing current practice, I believe that fewer women are ready to view themselves as doomed to social shame if they start an affair with an engaged man, or to irreparably submit to being forever a "second—or secondary-object" with a man ready to entertain a split double object choice. This is probably contributing to confronting men with more demanding partners. The difficulty in protracting the split brings about the phantasy of regression.

On the other hand, we see nowadays many young men who, when confronted with an increasing number of independent women who fall less easily into the categories or roles of the "idealised" or "debased" sexual object, are very worried about their manhood when a love relation comes up. Others tend to have mainly undifferentiated, friendly, "sibling-like" symbiotic relations, often including sex but hardly any passion or that particular quality that pertains to feelings of encountering a "special" object.

There seems to be a fairly widespread belief that women seek and tolerate fusional levels in love more than men who, as I have described above, can run into sexual defailances when confronted with fearful regressive trends. Is this true? And if so, why? While clinical evidence makes me side with those who believe that this is true, it is hard to formulate convincing theoretical explanations to justify it. I can think of a few; but objections to any of them are not easy to defeat.

Furthermore, I am well aware that many analysts have clinical evidence to prove that women can have as much difficulty as men in experiencing closeness and merging. And with very sound arguments as well, such as the fact that while men cannot conceal sexual defailance to themselves or their partners, women can feel and convey authentic participation to their partners whilst being uncertain as to whether they achieved orgasm or not. While this is undeniable, we could still argue that for most men the lack of erection or orgasm will be (consciously) experienced as equivalent to not making love, whilst for many women this is not the case at all, and the affectionate sensual foreplay can be felt as gratifying in its own right.

Merging and emerging experiences in intercourse within a love relation, carry the trace of the early self-object processes of individuation. The complex interweaving of regressive symbiotic trends as opposed to differentiation—with its necessary quota of aggressive drives in the service of growth—may fall short of a sufficiently adequate outcome and result in the defence of a regressive fusional experience that is part and parcel of genital sexuality in a love relationship.

A crucial issue that I think needs to be further explored is the problem of aggression underlying male impotence. The cases of occasional impotence that I came across in my practice (certainly not sufficient to allow for generalisations) regarded men who had healthy competitive drives at the service of work and personal achievement, while they were extremely passive and submissive with their regular partners.

This subject introduced in the analysis of X, an impotent patient (Amati Mehler, 1992), the theme of passive compliance with parental wishes at the cost of not recognising his own, except in regard to his professional development. X was deeply attached to his parents who had a very symbiotic relation between themselves and with their son (an undifferentiated triangle). He was able to defy his father, who would always warn him against striving for what appeared difficult or unrealistic professional goals, by achieving, in fact, in very successful intellectual and business enterprises. The patient's need to challenge whatever the father felt to be impossible, on one hand, inflated his omnipotence, but on the other it allowed him to achieve a partial release from an engulfing symbiosis that involved not only him and his mother but also the father, thus enhancing an even more generalised confusion of self-object boundaries and differentiated identifications. Seduction coupled with compliance had a considerable impact on management of frustration and aggression in his relation with his wife and other women with whom he carried on multiple affairs. But the anger that he roused in his partners, as well as the anger experienced by two women patients of mine over the repeated failure of their love partners, made me wonder.

These two women, otherwise sympathetic and understanding, after sharing excited foreplay with their partners whose erection dropped right before penetration, felt this defailance as a betrayal and an attack on the relationship. They felt that their partners would bring them to a state of blissful abandonment and then—as one of them said—leave her alone and without containment at the time when she felt that she was totally "losing herself". One of these female patients dreamed that she was in a cosy room with her partner, but suddenly the walls of their shared space fell apart; terrified, she felt as though she were floating in space without containment. The subjective experience of these female patients corresponded to, and mirrored, their partners' difficulties in letting themselves go, in losing control of the situation and sharing the sense of loss of boundaries. But, more relevant, was that there was the perception of a sort of miscarriage or displacement of the aggressive drive rather than it remaining at the service of attachment and bonding intimacy through penetration.

The experience of a complete, deep heterosexual intimacy implies tolerating regression and surrendering within genital intercourse, to the primary erotic-sensual affect, embedded in the oceanic totalising experience of symbiosis. This capacity is then related in its deepest layers to those processes which, generated along the development of separation-individuation processes, lead to gender identity, thus allowing not only recognition of the "other", but also identification with the "different" other. This is of the utmost importance if the merging experience in love, with the blurring of ego boundaries, is not to overlap with the earlier frightening and annihilating aspects of the sense of loss of the self, or to induce anxieties about one's own "maleness" or "femininity". Thus, a deep involving love relation is doomed to meet the bedrock of individual capacity for experiencing complete intimacy.

In a paper on gender identity, Argentieri (1990) remarks that "anatomy (or biology) is not destiny and is not in itself sufficient to guarantee adequate drive development or specific gender identity". Although one could hardly disagree with this, it is still important to detect whether and when anatomy, in its mental representation and fantasies, may determine the modality in which faulty processes of separation-individuation influence drive development and sexual life.

Ferenczi (1923) considers intercourse as a partial regression to intrauterine life, and wrote: "the male penetrates the female genital with his penis, which is a miniature representation of the ego". I would like to point here to the penis as the infantile version of the ego, because in my view it illustrates some of the clinical situations to which I am referring and indicates the need to identify deeper than phallic levels of castration anxiety, as was clearly expressed in the dream of a patient:

> I was in a place of thermal baths, a place a bit like a clinic, maybe for old people. The whole place was fenced and access to it was underground. It had a fantastic park and was a lovely place (the search for the lost "infantile paradise" had been a leitmotiv in previous sessions) and I was with a woman, don't know who. I looked through the window, inside the pavilions, and saw many naked women, white and plump, lying down with their little children. They are ill and it seems as if they could be disassembled, like, say, if you had a kidney that didn't work it would be dismantled, set by their side and remain connected to them—as if it were an artificial kidney or one in dialysis. But I wasn't sure if it was their organs or their children that were lying beside them ... I say to myself that probably those are their organs and they do not work properly ... Even if it's not a bloody situation, I think it' s horrible.

This oneiric image—in which this patient could not make out whether what lay close to the mothers' bodies were penises, mothers' organs, or babies—seems to me to illustrate precisely the core issue of what a symbiotic, merging experience represents for the cases that I am trying to illustrate. On one hand, it represents the wish to regain the "lost paradise" of complete reunion with the primary object, separation from which threatens survival and constitutes "the prototype of all castration", as Freud (1909) points out in a footnote added in 1926 to the case of "Little Hans". On the other hand, at a very deep level, the claustrophobic-like phantasies reveal fears related to the penis carrying along with it, during intercourse, all the body-self inside a woman, and concretely remaining a "hostage" inside a woman's body, just as a part of this patient had remained a psychological hostage of his mother.

Coming back to the relation between anatomy (or biology) and destiny, and to the debated question of whether women tolerate, more than men, the fusional levels in love, whatever the fear of closeness or merging experience may represent for them, the underlying symbiotic phantasies in which the anxiety is embedded—inasmuch as they are intimately connected to the mental representation of early body-mind interactions—could hardly be the same as those of men. A further complication is that part of the symbiotic tie of the little girl is carried over from the mother to the father, enhancing its longer duration as well as implying a difference in the process of retroactive re-signification (*Nachträglichkeit*) of early anxieties in relation to the primary objects. So, while women are bound to a much more difficult process of primary disidentification with the mother, a quota of fusional experience will physiologically "survive" the separation from her through normal investment in the father and male objects.

Men may relinquish primary identification and fusion with the mother more easily through identification with the father, but regressive merging experiences during intercourse with a woman can always risk bringing them closer to undifferentiation in which the fear of total re-engulfment (Anna Freud, 1952) is reactivated. In fact, (as I wrote elsewhere), impotence can be the herald of a great passionate love, but, paradoxically—as a last resort for survival—the fear of regression can also defeat love.

To conclude, we may wonder, what could the opposite situation entail, when no regression is feared—or even feasible—because there simply has been little differentiation, and when diversity, rather than being valued, is losing its socio-cultural meaning. I am not only wondering about the possible effects of this general maternal-paternal and male-female functional overlap on our theories, but I am concerned, on one hand, about issues of gender identity from an individual developmental viewpoint; on the other hand, it is hard not to speculate about the fate of male and female gender interactions, especially concerning *attraction* towards the "other" as separate and different. No difference implies no tension, but, rather, a narcissistic mirroring of oneself in the "same-other".

What will be the fate of *desire,* curiosity, and the wish to penetrate the mysteries of the unknown Other in the search for mature genital object love? I have no answers, only doubts and queries.

References

Amati Mehler, J. (1992). Love and male impotence. *International Journal of Psychoanalysis*, 73: 467–480.

Amati Mehler, J. (2012). *The Father* (in press).

Argentieri, S. (1990). Il sesso degli angeli. In: *Del Genere Sessuale.* Rome: Borla.

Betcher, W. & Pollack, W. (1993). *In a Time of Fallen Heroes: The Re-creation of Masculinity.* New York: Atheneum.

Ferenczi, S. (1923). *Thalassa: A Theory of Genitality.* New York: Psychoanalytic Quarterly, 1938.

Freud, A. (1952). A connection between the states of negativism and of emotional surrender (Hörigkeit). *International Journal of Psychoanalysis*, 33: 265.

Freud, S. (1909). Analysis of a five year old boy. *S. E., 10.* London: Hogarth.

Freud, S. (1910). A special type of object choice made by men. *S. E., 11.* London: Hogarth.

Freud, S. (1912). On the universal tendency to debasement in the sphere of love. *S. E., 11.* London: Hogarth.

Freud, S. (1930). *Civilization and its Discontents. S. E., 21.* London: Hogarth.

Klein, M. (1946). Notes on some schizoid mechanisms. In: *Envy and Gratitude and Other Works. Vol. 3.* London: Hogarth Press.

Sandler, J. (1959). The body as phallus: a patient's fear of erection. *International Journal of Psychoanalysis*, 40: 191–198.

Shweder, R. (1994). What do men want? A reading list for the male identity crisis. *The New York Times Book Review* (9 January): 3, 24.

CHAPTER SIX

Lack of discrimination as a defence mechanism

Martina Burdet Dombald

When thinking about masculine and feminine characteristics today, there came to my mind that grey area where there seems to be no clear discrimination between the masculine and the feminine. Neither masculine nor feminine. Androgynous. (The Oxford Concise Dictionary defines "androgyn" as "hermaphrodite, a human being combining characteristics of both sexes" whose external characteristics do not "correspond definitely to those of his/her own sex".) Unisex. An inevitable date with Narcissus. The same Narcissus as always, although the social interpretation of psychical conflict bears the signs of its times and its codes.

Two present-day figures that try to condense both masculine and feminine—in other words, to deny both the sexual as well as the gender difference—came to my mind. One, a character of a work that became a huge literary success, Lisbeth Salander, heroine of the trilogy *Millenium* written by the deceased Swedish author, Steig Larson. The other, that of a new pop star, Lady Gaga, a candidate for success on a par with Madonna or Michael Jackson.

The former is a skinny young girl of twenty-four, short in stature, with her face half covered by her black hair. She wears a leather jacket. Her figure is hardly distinguishable from that of a boy. With pierced eyebrows, tongue, nipples, navel, nose, and ears, and tattoos, among which a dragon crossing her back stands out, Lisbeth offers a profile which tends to the androgynous. She is bisexual and her relationships are dominated by her lack of emotion. She does not relate well to people. She feels extremely alone. Intelligent and alone, perhaps owing to traumas associated to a parental relationship in which her father used to abuse her mother. She suffers Asperger´s syndrome.

Stephani Joanne Angelica Germanotta chooses the pseudonym Lady Gaga—poker face—as in the title of one of her songs, in homage to Queen. (Note that G. Sand called herself George in Paris and Aurore in the provinces.) Like Lisbeth, she is bisexual and breaks away from dress conventions, neither masculine nor feminine. Basically fancy dress. She may well dress like a flower or like something out of a Martian space laboratory. She may wear a dress covered with slices of skin, as at a recent gala where she won awards for her music videos. A second skin? At times she even sowed the seed of doubt as to whether she was actually a hermaphrodite by emphasising the lips of her vagina as if it were a penis in a music video where she asks herself: "Does Lady Gaga have a penis … or … is she a hermaphrodite?" Neither man nor woman. She claims not to make love for fear of losing her power through her vagina.

Both figures seem to cross all boundaries, or desire to do so; they wish to avoid sexual differentiation, deny the anatomical differences between the sexes, and, quite clearly, ignore that of gender. (Briefly, by sexual difference I mean anatomical difference of the sexes, not that of the origin of sexual orientation nor desire nor the origin of the conviction of having a feminine or masculine identity, which are more related to gender, as described by Stoller.) They represent true social phenomena. The work by Steig Larson—a literary phenomenon. Various comments regarding the fictional heroine point to a "new heroine of the twentieth century", to a new feminism.

On the other hand, Lady Gaga is another mass phenomenon who beats all audience and sales records. (In December 2010, she performed in Madrid before a crowd of 7000 ecstatic young people between the ages of fifteen and thirty, driven into a frenzy by their idol.) These figures seduce everyone, or attempt to do so. "Seduce", indeed, with its etymological meaning of "allure". A performance of one of the original fantasies "Uhr Fantasien", a fantasy present from the beginning, described by Freud in his lecture XXIII, "Introduction to Psychoanalysis" (together with those of castration, primal scene, and return to the maternal womb).

How are we to interpret these phenomena, that I have taken as examples of present-day social reality, from a psychoanalytic point of view? Lisbeth Salander and Lady Gaga clearly advocate indifferent sex acceptable in two ways: indifferent sex in the sense of it being unimportant, as if the matter were indifferent—sex practised in the same way as one goes to the cinema, without emotion, sex practised the same with a woman as a man. And indifferent sex understood as lacking sexual differentiation, as a performance tending to unisex.

From a biological point of view, "masculine" and "feminine" allude to anatomical and physiological differences. However, the revolution attributed to psychoanalysis consists precisely in having removed sexuality from pure biology or anatomy in order to place the emphasis on fantasy, feelings, thoughts, and their transformation with relation to perception, versus non-perception, of the anatomical differences between the sexes. Psychosexual identity does not exist initially, it has to be constructed in both sexes. It becomes the product of the endowing with sexual difference, of its fantasies around this difference, and the complex play of identification with the parents, starting from a first and primary link with the feminine maternal being with its origins in both sexes.

Sexual indiscrimination, indifference, with all the shades of meaning that that infers, can be considered as re-editions of a narcissistic phallic completeness. Mythical Narcissus, indifferent. Indifferent to Echo. Indifferent to another self. In love with his reflection. The present indifference, worshipped and observed beneath some social phenomena that confuse sexual indiscrimination with having a phallus or narcissistic phallic completeness, which I have just mentioned, would be the same as past indifference. It belongs to the normal development of the individual and it may also become pathological. We could talk of an indiscrimination of life as opposed to an indiscrimination of death on the model of life narcissism versus death narcissism as proposed by André Green.

The lack of symmetry between the sexes implies different forms of desire, suffering, and loving in human development. It opposes the mythical idea of self, of the narcissistic wishes of lovers. I will focus this chapter on two specific questions:

1. Sexual undifferentiation, a theoretical hypothesis on the origins of sexuality, is also a normal phenomenon that is observed in adolescence as a rite of passage to the genital objectal love for a partner.

It implies a structurising, defensive "homo" moment against the distress of oedipal complex and fear of castration. Only if it lasts beyond this stage could it be considered from a more pathological angle proper to neurosis.

2. The lack of sexual differentiation as a consequence of the undifferentiation not achieved between ego/non-ego owing to early traumas and/or a structuring of the narcissistic self, with its clinging to a real life object, an attachment to an undifferentiated object, has little to do with the previous point. In this case we are facing a regression to a state of confusion proper to what for Freud would be the primary narcissism that acts as a defence against the distress of not being. The undifferentiation of ego/non-ego underlies undefined sexual problems because what is vital is to be able to vanquish a psychic individuality, to exist as subject.

The human subject, from a psychoanalytic perspective, is constituted bearing in mind a permanent conquest of differentiation at different levels: between the generations, between the sexes, between psychic applications. The difference of sex is the first of these differences, para-digmatic of all differences. It is how we enter the world. It is because of sexual difference that the other looks questioningly at the newborn baby. Every difference orders, controls. The sexual difference also points to that.

The child, from his perception of sexual difference, will begin to elab-orate sexual theories in order to elaborate the first difference that vio-lates his ego and his narcissism. Psycho-sexual identification is being constructed. Sexual difference invites us to think again of origins, the primary, the cause. Naturally the child is seen differently because of his sexual difference by the other. But from infancy, a time of undifferentia-tion before differentiation is postulated. The sexual is lived in an undif-ferentiated way in the sense that the child perceives the other as similar to himself. This is the moment of the primary narcissistic hypothesis postulated by Freud; the two elements in play are experienced as simi-lar elements. In primary narcissism, the other is undifferentiated in what relates to his sex. (Freud writes in "The ego and the id", (1923), that the child behaves the same with both sexes, perceives his parents to be the same as himself and the same as each other).

Does the pulsion sprout from the other or the self? Like many writ-ers, I believe there is a permanent dialectic between the infant and the other responsible for binding the pulsion. "The object creates and unites the pulsion. And the pulsion creates and unites the object" states Cruz-Roche (2006). Although Freud does not link it, the economic problem is closely linked to the external other. It sprouts simultaneously from inside and outside, it sprouts from an inner exterior. It satisfies the pulsion and becomes part of the subject. It is precisely through the defects in the meeting between the psyche and the world, called other, or Other with a capital "O", that the necessary bonding guaranteeing the success of the first bonding, identical to primary erogenous masochism, fails. The shortcomings of the primary object as a pulsional vehicle, according to many writers, with whom I agree, is the pulsion of death.

Initially, contemporary with primary narcissism, the phase of primary homosexuality prevails (Denis, 2005; Schaeffer, 2005) as an erotic investiture of the seductive mother in the loving exchange with her son. Sexuality leads to an object similar to self. Feminine for both sexes, of course. And this will last up to the time of the experience of perception of sexual differences with all its important dynamic consequences: elaboration of the primal scene, posterior elaboration of the Oedipus complex. (We see its rejection in fetishism).

In the phase of latency and adolescence, there is a return to a kind of sexual undifferentiation. (This may well explain the seductive aspect of the Lady Gagas or Lisbeth Salanders who try to seduce girls as well as boys, homos as well as heteros). Defence, in this phase of development, contrasted with the couple as a union of two different individuals, which is perceived as threatening, because it compels questions about the Oedipus complex and castration. Defence of the homo—similar-homogenerational—homosexual—constitutive of social ties that escape oedipal prohibitions, fear of castration, and generational inferiority.

This has to do with what is described by Braunschweig and Fain as *"anteros"*, that is to say, sexuality between similar individuals that coheres the group. Here the undifferentiation between the sexes is desired, organised. It is a kind of "homo-sexuality indifferent to sex" (Denis, 2005, p. 129) in the sense that there is no preference. The sex is unimportant and thus protects as much from exclusion from the primal scene as from generational inferiority. It is a defence against the fear of difference. In "Introduction to Narcissism", Freud (1914) considered the narcissistic choice of object as a *necessary* stage of development: the subject chooses first himself as the object of love and then chooses the object.

The cult of indifference, or of indiscrimination of the sexes, is no more than a defence used by psychism to protect itself when facing acute two-fold distress: that of castration and exclusion from the primal scene in predominantly neurotic patients; of dissolution when faced with the absence of differentiation ego/non-ego owing to early traumas and/ or problems that threaten with constructing a structurising narcissism in borderline patients. I have mentioned the former. Of the latter, I will now give some characteristics peculiar to borderline pathologies.

In borderline pathology, uppermost is the fear of fragmentation, dissolution into the other. It has not been possible to construct the differentiation between self and other, and the predominating distress is that of not being, sexual indiscrimination corresponding to another type of accident.

Difference/indifference, as masculine/feminine, as self/other, go in twos. Since the genesis the human being is born with the mark in his body of its sexuality, which does not necessarily correspond to his gender. Nonetheless, he is born with that mark. When the androgynous is not even conscious and the *con*-fusion between sexes has to do with a pregenital festival that is in reality the last desperate cry of aspiration for an outline of differentiated self, we are facing pathological forms of expression that speak of a defect in the structurisation of narcissism (the negative narcissism of André Green), of bonds marked by a melancholic function, by traumatic situations, by defects marked by a failure of the role of other in the first bonding constituted by the primary masochistic nucleus in Rosenberg´s theorisation going back to Freud, etc.

The way out of indiscrimination, of confusion, is traced via the creation of a primal scene fantasy, a primal scene that constitutes the origin from which identification and oedipal complex are elaborated. However, should there be a defect in the primary object responsible for making the first bonding understood as primary erogenous masochism, the functions enabling excitations will be made invalid, opening the way to a split ego, excessive excitement, the experience of void, psychosomatic problems, or to psychosis.

It is the mother, the primary object, who is the first other to be responsible for the first bonding between pulsions of life and death. It is also she who introduces father to son to the third (other of the object). Her desire´s other, the lover´s censure (Braunschweig & Fain). If this does not come about, he will remain anchored in the primary homosexuality contemporary of primary narcissism, a prisoner of a narcissistic phallic maternal image, or here, in a terminology that tries to highlight the precocious, archaic bisexual being (Schaeffer, 2005), like the sphinx at the doors of Thebes. Bisexual pregenital imago of a mother who has everything. It has everything: penis, babies, faeces. It is a pregenital "character" which has no sex, yet has all of them. It implies omnipotence, having everything. It is the "pregenital mammal" that Fain speaks sarcastically about. Imago of "disturbing strangeness" belonging to a world before words. It is the world of Freud´s "undifferentiated parents", of Klein´s "combined parents". We are in the phase "narcissistic stoppage" described by Racamier (1987), understood as a phase of blockage in the phase of mother-baby seduction from which the third (other) is excluded; we are in the phase of alienation within the other self, in the mother as champion of the law according to the referential schema chosen.

In reality, the rejection of sexual difference, as Freud noted, also emerges as a defence of the feminine in both sexes. However, in my opinion, the most important issue is that the impossibility of establishing the primal scene fantasy implies renouncing the Oedipus complex. If there is no representation of difference, neither will there be of separation or difference of the sexes, thus there will be neither castration nor separation.

The two paradigms that emerge from Freud´s work help us understand better the types of distress we try to avoid. The contemporary hysteria model of the first topography shows more clearly the specifically neurotic conflict. However, starting from the theorising on narcissism and from "Mourning and melancholy" (1915) Freud offers us another useful tool with the paradigm of sorrow marked by loss in order to understand narcissistic pathologies and problems related to the impossible elaboration of loss.

The real differentiation between masculine and feminine, the recognition of otherness in the difference of sex comes about in puberty but it presumes an accident-free pathway which at the same time presumes also a phallic stage for both sexes. We will see, however, in clinical cases, predominantly in borderline states, how there is a return to situations of undifferentiation, indiscrimination with the object.

To complete the examples chosen from our present-day social reality that I gave at the beginning, I will give two clinical examples: the former peculiar to a neurosis, the latter characteristic of a borderline case.

Mr. Bo is beautiful like David Bowie, like David Beckham whose photograph stood out in a thematic exhibition on beauty in Madrid (2010). He enjoys and takes pleasure in a Lacanian sense in his profile, which we could call androgynous. He is liked equally by men and women. He never loves and desires little. He only wishes to be liked by anyone—man or woman. As soon as he notices that he is liked, which is systematic and in every situation, he describes himself as if he were "a woman, dancing ballet steps". When alone, without a partner, he feels helpless and goes mad in his attempt to be liked even though to achieve this he has to suffer anguish in his return to the sick hell of "perfection and complete shit". He had lived having a phallus both as mummy and daddy. Although very successful in numerous fields, he ends up failing himself for not being "the Wonder". The Ideal. The Being. Bo flees castration and the distress of the excluded third other. Narcissism in neurosis.

Lola, my second example, illustrates dramatically a sexual confusion, the consequence of a traumatic display of parental primal scene. She rejects sexual difference, the "sex thing" as she calls it. One can observe perfectly that the anatomical difference of the sexes does not exist for her. She has other foci of concern and distress. Indeed, for a long time, this woman was dominated by a lack of bonding in Green's sense, the desire to not desire described by Aulagnier, in order to counteract the fear provoked by the distress of not being, feeling confused with the other self—a fact causing much distress; sexual indiscrimination prevails (like the buying of a whole cabbage so that the greengrocer does not know that you live alone) because her problem consists of defining a boundary that differentiates self from a primary object that she feels swallowed up by.

I will give only a few examples of her traumatic dreams that are valid as showing action or release, dreams of "an evacuative nature seeking a continent" (Paz, 2009): "I am in a bar, I put a meat sandwich in my vagina, which reminds me of my mother who cooks this meat. It makes me happy and I think it's nothing but a hole, as if the food satisfies the vagina". Another dream: "There's a bishop and one of my uncles who is showing his crotch, I want something from him but it's not sex because he's a bishop … Or two homosexual men who are kissing and that excites me, but if they are homosexual, it has nothing to do with me". Lola also dreams about penises … She has no awareness of sexual differences, she functions at a level of pre-genital fantasies.

Her terror, which she calls her "excitement in the head that goes Vu … Vu … Vu …", the way she explains how she goes from one idea to another, with no delay possible, fearing that she will go crazy, rejects sexual difference because of traumatism.

Conclusion

I wish to evoke—and hope I have managed to do so—different forms of sexual indiscrimination that lead from structuralised narcissistic figures in normal development of sexuality to forms of pathological narcissism. I have tried to distinguish the different kinds of distress dealt with through problems related to narcissism, according to what we may find in the field of neurosis or the more serious pathologies that we find on the road towards psychosis. I will conclude with this apt quote from Schaeffer (2005, p. 119): "Thought is the thought of difference". Without difference, I would add, there is no thought.

References

Braunschweig, D. & Fain, M. (1971). *Eros etantéros*. Paris:Petite Bibliothèque Payot.

Cruz-Roche, R. (2006). Excitación objetal y constitución del psiquismo. *Revista de psicoanálisis de la APM*. 48.06.

Denis, P. (2005). Narcisse indifférent. In : J. André (Ed.), *Les sexes indifférents*. Paris: Presses Universitaires de France.

Freud, S. (1914). On narcissism: an introduction. *S. E., 14*. London: Hogarth.

Freud, S. (1915). Mourning and melancholia. *S. E., 14*. London: Hogarth.

Freud, S. (1916). Lecture XXIII: The paths to the formation of symptoms. *S. E., 16*. London: Hogarth.

Freud, S. (1923). The ego and the id. *S. E., 14*. London: Hogarth.

Paz, J. C. (2009). Techno-cultural convergence: wanting to say everything, wanting to watch everything (Trans. Margaret Schwartz) *Popular Communication: The International Journal of Media and Culture*, 7: 130–139.

Racamier, P. -C. (1987). *De la perversion narcissique, Gruppo, no. 3* [On narcissistic perversion]. *Perversité dans les familles* [Perversity in families]. Paris: Clancier-Guénaud.

Schaeffer, J. (2005). Quelle différence de sexe. In: J. André (Ed.), *Les sexes indifférents*. Paris: Presses Universitaires de France.

CHAPTER SEVEN

Listening to psychical bisexuality in analysis

Teresa Rocha Leite Haudenschild

Introduction

For analysts to be able to listen to the psychical bisexuality of their analysands it is necessary for them to have a sufficiently elaborated psychobisexuality, that is, to have "a good internalised parental couple", which presupposes the differentiation of gender and generations. From this internal reference the analyst may hear the internal "failures" of their analysands: insufficient internalisation of a maternal or paternal figure, for instance (Ogden, 1991) insufficiency that is often due to transgenerational factors, "failures" in the constitution of the psychism of the parents of these analysands, which is noted extensively by Guignard (1996). Beyond its use in analytical listening, the psychobisexuality of the analyst will demarcate the reconstitution of the analysand's psychical bisexuality, both at the primary level (the level of mother-child primary relation) and the secondary level (related to Oedipal conflicts).

Constitution of psychical bisexuality

"Bisexuality is a masculine-feminine conjunction: a psycho-corporal-sexual 'complex' that, by principle, over time becomes more and more psychical, however, always maintains bonds with the body" (Haber, 1997, p. 66). How is it constructed? We can assume that from the beginning, before even being born, the child, as an object of desire of the couple, may be expected by them as having a determined sex. The newborn child is identified by the parents—and particularly by the mother (or not)—as a separated subject, "other", and thus designated (Stoller, 1968) as a sexual subject, with a determined gender. Therefore, throughout this process, the unconscious and conscious fantasies of the parents are of great significance, as is the elaboration or integration (or not) of their psychical bisexuality.

Primary psychical bisexuality

In the primary relation with the mother the child constructs its own primary psychical bisexuality. Bion (1962) says that the mother who is open to hearing everything that comes from the child, the mother capable of reverie, offers continence to the feelings, anguish, and desires of the child, naming them and exploring their meanings, as a favourable object, so that the child introjects the capacity of containment of its own psychical content. For Bion therefore, there is a first moment in which the child borrows, without noticing, the mother's capacity for containment, which gradually becomes introjected by the child, and a second moment in which the child, already capable of self-containment, is able to use it.

Winnicott (1966, p. 177) states that at the very first moment "the object is the subject". The mother adapts herself to the baby in such a way that the child feels that the breast is their continuity. The breast is a subjective object, "the first object, the object not yet repudiated as a not-me phenomenon" (p. 177). In this primary illusion, in this mode of object relation with a pure female element, the experience of being is established, the most fundamental experience of a human being. "Projective and introjective identifications both stem from this place where each is the same as the other" (p. 177). In a second instance, when the child has already realised this primary identification of being one with the breast, it may build relationships from the pure male element: the child may be an active or passive subject in relation to the other, with its own investments, in everything it does.

Winnicott (1966) points out that in the initial moment of the experience of being "here one finds a true continuity of generations, being which is passed on from one generation to another, via the female element of men and women and of male and female infants" (p. 177). In this transmission mediated by a pure female element, as Winnicott affirms, I believe that there already exists, in this contact with the being of the mother, an apprehension of the mother's psychical bisexuality, the apprehension of the value that she gives to all human beings, be they male or female. If not, how could she open herself, without restrictions, to the relation of continuity with the baby of a sex other than her own? It is my understanding that the mother capable of psychical listening through her reverie, and the mother capable of adapting to the baby's needs, must have a reasonable elaboration of her own psychical bisexuality, resulting from a "good internalised parental relationship". If in the first moment the initial relation of the mother and her child is "neutral", as Winnicott says, this can only be because her feminine sexual investments are directed at her husband, while the maternal investments are directed at the child (Haudenschild, 2003).

Secondary psychical bisexuality

The secondary psychical bisexuality originates from the primary psychical bisexuality, from the perception by the child that its mother has an "other look", different from the primary maternal dedicated to it, for an "other" object: the father. It is this perception of the "primary feminine" (Guignard, 1997) by the child that marks its sexuality: the real way in which the mother lives her own sexuality, together with the child's own fantasies and envy. (This perception of the "primary feminine" of the mother by the baby is different to Winnicott's concept of a "pure female element" which corresponds to the "primary maternal" relationship of Klein.) Here the transgenerational becomes evident (Haudenschild, 2005): the transmission of the value given to the father by the mother, of the contentment in intercourse with him, (which presupposes a transmission from the grandmother to the mother) all of which is indelibly marked on the psychical structure of the child, whether that child be a boy or a girl.

The elaboration of the psychical secondary bisexuality, related to passion, anger, and oedipal rivalry (positive and negative) is coloured as much by parental imagos, which result from the elaboration of primary bisexuality, as by real experiences the child has in the relationship with its parents, whose investments also carry weight. The secondary psychical bisexuality refers to the relationships with total objects, to the depressive position and oedipal conflicts, presupposing a communication inter and intra psychical at the level of the symbolic.

Psychical bisexuality in the clinic

Bion states that (1965, p. 143): "if analysis has been successful in restoring the personality of the patient he will approximate to being the person he was when his development became compromised". He believes, therefore, that everyone, given that they do not have organic prejudice, has the innate tools for psychical development. However, as the mind "does not grow like a flower" (Meltzer, 1989), and since it is constituted in the relationship, and initially constructed through the primary relation with the mother, we have to ask what conditions are sufficient in order for this to occur. In this "primary feminine" relationship the child perceives the feminine look of the mother to a masculine "other": the father.

As we see, for Bion, the mother capable of reverie, the mother able to give emotional meaning to the primitive experiences of her child, is fundamental to the mental constitution of the baby. She is a post-oedipal mother, with "a good internalised couple", who has mental space for the father, for the other, and the different. According to Bion, analysts themselves must be like this mother capable of reverie: able to receive, to name, and to give meanings, none of which are ever saturated, to the emotional experiences that arise in the relationship the analysand has with the analyst in the session. Bion further emphasises, when he talks of the mother capable of reverie, that, beyond the love for the baby, the love she has for the father is essential in the relationship she has with her child. In terms of the analyst we can think of the love for the truth, the unknown, which will be unveiled (*aletheia*) in the relationship, each day anew ... The love of the analyst for psychoanalysis, to which he/she is the servant, gives way to the psychic life.

Psychical bisexuality of the analyst in the session

How does listening happen in the analysis? What is the configuration of internal objects that will allow the analyst to listen to their analysand? We must think of this listening as a wide fan ranging from listening to primitive mental states, such as those related to the attraction to sensorial points and adhesive relations studied and described by Esther

Bick (1968, 1986) and Meltzer (1975) prior to the paranoid-schizoid position, to more evolved states related to total objects and the depressive position. The analyst, in analysis, requires a mental range at all these levels to a sufficient degree in order to be able to help his or her analysand to access them too. However, we know well that we are often called, in some analytical processes, to access within ourselves obscure corners of our minds that have never before been explored, to discover hidden truths never before revealed.

Analytical listening to the psychical bisexuality

For Bion, what helps us in this courageous enterprise alongside our analysands is our "good internal couple", our primary psychical bisexuality (Haber, 1997), internalised ever since the primary relationships with our mother. The mother herself carries her own internalised parents (Guignard, 1997), coloured (or not) by the love and value she has for her husband and vice versa. We analysts work from this basic identification—the fruit that grew from the loving connection of a couple that valued us, and that attributed to us our gender identity based on our bodies (Stoller, 1966), that respected our mysterious psychical singularity, and invited us to respect the singularity of the couple as much as the individuals involved.

On the couch, when an analysand, through his or her phantasmatic representations, makes explicit a maternal unconscious that expresses a failed heterosexual encounter (for example, that of a woman who is submissive to her husband or who makes him submit phallically), we can certainly hypothesise that in this analysand a bisexual failure in the integration and internalisation of the parental couple comes from a basic failure in their identity at an initial stage where a healthy narcissism might have been established. It is clear that to listen deeply and accurately to the unconscious of our analysands, it is necessary for us to have spent some years in analytical work, given that the primary difficulties in the constitution of psychical bisexuality only appear long after the secondary difficulties, which are manifested from the beginning of the analysis.

Listening to psychical bisexuality in the clinic

Two analysands come to mind: Marina and Andrea. Both were the last children born in their respective families: the "leftovers", the child who was not part of the parent's plans. Both women are high-flying executives, the first around forty, the second thirty years old, successful professionally, and both with a husband and a single child. What is astonishing at the beginning of the analysis of both is, despite their willingness to lie on the couch, they have great difficulty in bringing free associations and dreams to the sessions. They stick to objective everyday problems in relationships with work colleagues or their husbands.

Marina: being the "man" of the house so as not to suffer

Over time, Marina brings a memory that her mother, when a baby, was almost killed by her great grandmother (who was the mother-in-law of Marina's grandmother), the motive being that Marina's mother was the third girl (as Marina is too), yet another mouth to feed, and furthermore, not a man who would be able to work to support the family. The great grandmother put the baby outside one night during winter while her daughter-in-law slept; however, her son, Marina's grandfather, awoke and saved Marina's mother's life. Up till this point in her life, Marina had lived lamenting her lack of creativity (which was real, and only with a great deal of effort was she able to achieve professional success) and from this point in the analysis onwards, her life gained a new fluency.

I believe that it was the memory of her grandfather saving her mother that brought her a more stable integration of an internalised caring couple, the basis for her identity, an integration that refers to her primary psychical bisexuality. Here was a man who protected his daughter's life, letting his wife focus on dedicating herself to her child without having to worry. This was the choice that Marina's mother made: she chose a husband who was dedicated to his daughters and loving. Despite this, based on many years of analysis, my hypothesis is that this mother had a failed heterosexual encounter with her husband, dedicating herself more to the function of mother than of wife. It was Marina, for example, who went arm in arm with her father to the church as a teenager, while her mother prepared the Sunday lunch. Moreover, Marina was sure that the father was having a long term extramarital affair. Furthermore, still under the transgenerational shadow that "girls are just another unwanted mouth to feed", Marina greatly appreciated looking like her father, often wearing masculine clothes. Despite that, one of her most treasured memories that arose at this moment in the analysis, was of her mother making a very feminine dress for her and her oldest sister, cut from the same material: "it was of organza, scratchy (it hurts to be a woman), but I was so content. I still have a photo of myself wearing it".

Andrea: the pain of not being accepted

Andrea had a mother who was very submissive and a phallic father who was susceptible to sudden attacks on his wife and daughters, but who always protected the only son, the brother born immediately before Andrea. Andrea says that her mother never protected her from her father's rage, which was expressed particularly violently when she, at sixteen, got her first job with the aim of saving to travel during her holidays.

Failures in the constitution of primary psychical bisexuality

We can surmise that the couple internalised by Marina and Andrea's parents had a great intergenerational influence on the parental couple internalised by both women. The devaluation of women, internalised by both through the unconscious and conscious relationship with the parental couple, made them, at an early stage, seek out financial success in order to free themselves from submission to men. Furthermore, the mark of this devaluation weighed heavily on the choice of their partners: both, lacking in initiative, were sustained by them to a great extent.

I believe they made these choices due to a fear of being dominated, as their mothers did, but also through a longing to reconstruct the early relationship with the mother, where these men offer a symbiotic relationship, of sensorial care and constant presence (either these women are like daughters of their husbands, or their husbands are like their own sons): a relationship which these husbands in fact maintain with their own mothers, even today. Marina and Andrea slide around in this vicious cycle at the beginning of the analysis: the need for economic independence, but also an unconscious submission to a symbiotic primary relation, not subjectified, transmitted in the primary relation with the mother. It was necessary, therefore, to listen to the failures in the constitution of their primary bisexuality, constitutive of their identities. This, without forgetting that, over the years, my listening, as that of a post-oedipal mother capable of reverie, gradually allowed listening to the new, the different, introducing the place of the father and favouring the internalisation of the caring couple. I believe that for Marina the memory of the grandfather saving her mother has been the fruit of an acceptance and recognition of the place of the father, through introjections of the parental couple in the analytical partnership.

Marina and Andrea's journey

Marina, having had more time in analysis, shows clear psychic growth, freely associates and brings dreams with extremely interesting elaborations; and her relationships with her husband and daughter have undergone considerable modification, permitting growth and allowing each member of the family to choose his or her own path.

Andrea is still going through "pains of her own psychic gestation". She is discovering how much, and to what extent, the defensive armour of her professional success has been built up to defend herself from the men she has to live with on a daily basis, as she is a director at a large business where there are few women. What guides her analysis is her love of the truth, revealed in her spontaneity and her courage in suffering psychical pain, retaking initial steps in her development through naming and giving meaning to early states which for a long time have been encapsulated, waiting to be listened to by someone capable of receiving them (Freud, 1937). In the consulting room, parallel to their scholarly successes, the pain appears of not feeling loved by their mother, "who only had eyes for her brother". The shame of feeling like "one more girl", being passed down the clothes of older sisters ... The pain of the non-presence of the father, always away from home, busy with lovers, while mother submitted as he sustained the home.

Gradually, Andrea talks of her maternal grandparents who lived close to home, and she recalls her fights with her parents, which were frequent: "I was really foul-mouthed and always answered back to my mother or my father, when they wanted me to give in without reason". These grandparents listened to her and dried her tears (Andrea still cries frequently upon retelling her own misfortunes: it's a mute cry, sometimes almost imperceptible) and she says that she always "left her grandparent's house a different person". She left whole, I think, for this couple listened to the "other" in her—her singularity—and helped her reconstruct the primary internalised couple, her primary psychical bisexuality, basic to her self-esteem and her own identity. The memory of this caring couple also appeared after some time in the analytical partnership, presupposing that she expresses the more stable internalisation of this couple.

Failures in the constitution of the secondary psychical bisexuality

Here, the conflict expressed takes its starting point from the unconscious fantasies of the subject herself, and not from real traumatic situations occurring during infancy, nor transgenerational unconscious fantasies (alienating identifications). "This is characteristic of a psychism organized by the depressive position and Oedipal fantasies, whose function belongs to the symbolic order" (Haber, 1997, p. 65). In this case we may think of a classic analysis and the installation of a "neurosis of transference", where the negative and positive oedipal conflicts with each of the parents and with the couple would appear over time, just as with sibling rivalries. These are conflicts that are related to "total objects", directed at total people, who have their own personalities. The secondary bisexuality is articulated with the primary, since it is a transformation of the latter.

Articulation of primary and secondary psychical bisexuality

Thus, in a person who has not yet established a firm primary psychical bisexuality, their conflicts—search for recognition and value, pain of being unloved, desire for symbiotic affection, and so on—may colour the oedipal elaboration. The primary bisexuality may in this way, "après coup", gain a rereading and a re-elaboration. Due to the fact that these early stages will only be able to be explored further on in the process of analysis, the conflicts related to secondary bisexuality are the first to be approached in the analysis.

It is from the attentive and recognising parental look to femininity or masculinity that the sexual identity of the child is constituted. If the mother or father should be anguished in relation to the sex of the other, if there is a reciprocal depreciation or devaluation, then the child will introject this couple that do not adjust and that do not accept heterosexuality, which will lead to a failure in the constitution of the primary psychical bisexuality, as we have seen.

Failures in the constitution of the secondary psychical bisexuality occur when the child is unable to introject an adequate couple due to his or her own envy, or an inability to accept his or her limitations, implicated in the renunciation of qualities, attributes and privileges of the other sex.

The "pregnant" boy

I recall a three-year-old analysand, whose mother was pregnant. On arriving for the first analytic encounter, he told me that he was expecting a baby who was going to be born before that of his mother. He expanded his belly and put my hand on it so that I could feel how big his baby was. He said that he was going to breastfeed it when it was born, because his breasts were going to grow bigger than his mother's and he would have much more milk than her. This boy, as I see it, had very clear masculine identifications with a designation of gender given by the parents, and a "good internalised couple". However, he was going through polymorphic perverse fantasies in accordance with his age, developing negative and positive oedipal elaborations, and working through the renunciation of ambisexuality. Despite believing in his own infantile sexual theories, it was possible for him to renounce them quite rapidly, in the analysis, through his entrance in school and playing with other boys (he was the only child and until this moment had only lived among adults and predominantly with his mother).

The first-time father who is a "mother" to his son

An adult analysand also comes to mind who had just had his first child, but who thought his partner was incapable of caring for the child (despite telling me that she had put aside all her professional achievements and was breastfeeding the child). He took a number of weeks off work and was always present to take care of the child, giving baths, rocking the baby to sleep, in short, substituting his partner. He would say, "The only thing I don't have is milk, but I think if I had to, I would: I read that in Africa there's a group that, when the mother dies, the father gives milk to the newborn child—look at how the head rules the body ..." Interpretations of how he wanted to have feminine attributes were not heard, but were sometimes transformed by him into eulogies of his own maternal qualities. He (also the first son) began renouncing, with great difficulty, the desire to occupy the place of both sexes, only recognising over time the difference and value of his own woman. Even the value of the analyst (a woman) was checked: "Don't you think a man would understand me better?"

However, to my mind, with a sufficiently established primary psychical bisexuality, he, envious of the attributes of the feminine body, had the fantasy of a man as a complete being: enough for him to want to take the place of his woman, the mother. As I understand it, admiring maternal attributes, and envying the attention given by the mother to his sister, who came soon after he did, he tried to form a "homo" pair with his son, leaving out the woman (just as he had felt left out when his mother primarily looked after his newborn sister).

Re-elaborations of the primary psychical bisexuality always appear later, because the elaboration of a secondary psychical bisexuality originates from the primary. It falls to the analyst to decide when the predominance of failures in the elaboration are of one or the other, so as to direct focus and interpretation at the appropriate level.

Final considerations

Some years ago I conducted research into analytical listening based on the gender of the analyst and the analysand (Haudenschild, 2001). One of the interesting details encountered was the difficulty of male analysts to apprehend the erotic transference of analysands who were women, the majority interpreting them from a maternal position, as if these investments were those of a small child responding to the mother. Marked by Kleinian, Winnicottian, and Bionian influences, analysts today cannot put to one side the marked influence of the mother in the constitution of their own psychism and that of their analysands. Today, listening from the maternal position is often favoured to the detriment of others, just as Freud, in his time, favoured the paternal transferences and practically "did not hear" the maternal. Nevertheless, it was Freud himself who, with the fundamental psychoanalytic concept of "fluctuating attention" (Freud, 1912), opened the doors to immeasurable ways of listening and to a position for the analyst that is never fixed.

It is as though the analyst opens up to an unpredictable and improvised choreography, beginning from the minimal movements of the analysand, and at the same time maintaining a third eye, at a distance, like the director of a scene in a film, inviting his or her partner to contact nuances of the truth present in the relation. A truth frequently camouflaged and distorted by defences constructed and maintained over years, sometimes a whole life, like fortresses. In order to get to know them, and help the analysand find a way to leave them, we must often "dance" with the analysand for some time, according to his or her choreography, until we reach an understanding of why he or she is confined there, far from the real possibilities of life. We are invited "to dance" by each one of our analysands and, as partners and attentive observers, we are able to help them re-elaborate their psychical bisexuality, the indispensable antidote to ambisexuality (Haudenschild, 2007). The acceptance that we can have both sexes in our psyche is what allows for the renouncement of having them bodily and leads us to perceive that masculine and feminine complete each other reciprocally.

Summary

To be able to listen to a patient's psychical bisexuality presupposes that the analyst must have a sufficiently elaborated psychical bisexuality too. I underlined that despite the fact the secondary psychical bisexuality appears first in the analysis it is a transformation of the primary that should be the focus of careful analytical work. I also emphasised the importance of the transgenerational in failures of the constitution of primary psychical bisexuality. As an extreme consequence of these failures, ambisexuality can occur in the place of psychical bisexuality.

References

Bick, E. (1968). The experience of the skin in early object relations. *International Journal of Psycho-Analysis*, 49: 484–486.

Bick, E. (1986). Further considerations on the function of the skin in early object relations. Findings from infant observation integrated into child and adult analysis & commentary by Donald Meltzer. *British Journal of Psychotherapy*, 2: 292–299.

Bion, W. (1962). A theory of thinking. In: *Second Thoughts*. London: Heinemann, 1967.

Bion, W. (1965). *Transformations*. London: Heinemann.

Freud, S. (1912). Recommendations to physicians practising psycho-analysis. *S. E., 12*. London: Hogarth.

Freud, S. (1937). Constructions in analysis. *S. E., 23*. London: Hogarth.

Guignard, F. (1996). *Au vif de l'infantile*. Lausanne: Delachaux et Niestlé.

Guignard, F. (1997). Le sourire du chat. In: *Épître à l'objet*. Paris: PUF.

Haber, M. (1997). Identité, bisexualité psychique et narcissisme. In: *Bisexualité: Monographies de la revue française de psychanalyse*. Paris: PUF.

Haudenschild, T. (2001). Gênero y proceso analítico. In: A. M. Alizade, M. Araújo & M. Gus (Eds.), *Masculino-Femenino*. Buenos Aires: Lumen, 2004.

Haudenschild, T. (2003). The green continent: the constitution of femininity in a clinical case. In: A. M. Alizade (Ed.), *Studies on Femininity*. London: Karnac.

Haudenschild, T. (2005). O poder das identificações alienantes relativas ao gênero. *Revista Brasiliera Psicanálise*, 39: 25.

Haudenschild, T. (2007). Dois em um. *Psicanálise em Revista*, Recife, 7: 95–104.

Meltzer, D. (1975). Adhesive identification. *Contemporary Psychoanalysis*, 11: 289–310.

Meltzer, D. (1989). Desenvolvimento recente do modelo da mente e sua relação com os sonhos na prática clínica, Rev. IDE, vol. 18.

Ogden, T. (1991). O limiar do complexo de édipo masculino. *Ide (São Paulo)*, 20: 38–49,199.

Stoller, R. J. (1966). The mother's contribution to infantile transvestic behaviour. *International Journal of Psycho-Analysis*, 47: 384–395.

Stoller, R. (1968). *Sex and Gender*. New York: Science House.

Winnicott, D. (1966). The splitting of male and female elements to be found in men and women. In: *Psycho-analytic explorations*. London: Karnac.

CHAPTER EIGHT

Masculinity and the analytic relationship—transforming masculinity in the course of the analysis

Rui Aragão Oliveira

In psychoanalysis, reflection on the constructs "father" and "mother" has determined the formulation of fundamental psychic functions, whose consequences affect the whole process of the child's mental development, being psychic functions differentiating constituents of masculinity and femininity. The affective contact with the father, as a third element, allows for intrapsychic experimentation of representing a significant other, outside the mother-baby dyad, thus providing the child with a separate and different mental space, which can promote the understanding of his/her own identity. This becomes a process that, beginning tumultuously during childhood, remains accentuated throughout the school and adolescent years, when emotional individuation takes place. It is current knowledge that such a process will accompany the individual throughout his/her life cycle (Diamond, 2004). The particular aspects of this triangular dynamic, and the identifications that accompany it, present themselves as structuring for the mental world, and for the masculine trajectories.

Freud showed the extraordinary implications of the oedipal experience and of the complex identificatory mechanisms in the establishment of masculinity (Freud, 1908, 1908a, 1913, 1921, 1923). Thus, masculinity would be associated, on the one hand, to separation from the mother as an incestuous object and, on the other hand, to the identification with the father figure.

Also, studies by Ferenczi, Klein, Mahler, Winnicott, and others on the psyche's earliest stages, allowed a deeper and differentiating understanding of the configuration of masculinity, in the dynamics of the mental world.

Referring to the early genital organisation, Melanie Klein describes the early Oedipus complex (Klein, 1928), which emerges as a consequence of the oral frustrations (with weaning) and the anal frustrations (with the learning of the first hygiene habits), and of the acknowledgment of the father's existence. Klein proposed that the Oedipus complex was triggered by the maternal body and its contents, which she named the feminine phase—in Alicia Etchegoyen's words: "During the anal-sadistic stage of libidinal development, in the second year, she believed that both the boy and girl showed an interest in the mother's body and its contents—initially faeces, but later on differentiated as other part-objects, such as babies, breast, penis, etc" (Etchegoyen, 2002, p. 25). In this feminine phase, the child fantasises the mother's body as full of good things, identifying her/himself with it. The knowledge of the father's penis, as a special content of the mother's body, introduces the Oedipus complex. Klein, at first, argues that the boy will want to destroy the father's penis to seize the mother's body (Etchegoyen 2002); whereas, the girl will identify herself with the mother's body that receives the father's penis. The early oedipal configuration appears, therefore, as related to the mother's body, and to the associated fantasies about partial objects (i.e., milk, food, father's penis, babies, etc.). Therefore, the child's relationship with the breast acquires a special significance, in that it is able to configure the oedipal conflict. It is the frustration, provided by the breast (inherent in the paranoid-schizoid anxiety), and the desire to repair it (associated with depressive anxiety), which allows the child to turn to the father's penis and thus access the triangular oedipal situation. Klein calls this important passage "the passage from the breast to the penis".

The basic anxiety, for both the boy and the girl, is due to the pursuit and guilt resulting from the destructive fantasies towards the mother's body (especially her breast), the father's penis, and the primal scene. When the child grows, he/she will perceive the father as a separate individual, finally allowing the organisation of the configuration described by Freud, through the transformation of the primal fantasy.

Klein states that the boy's castration anxiety and the girl's fear of losing the love of the object are secondary, as both derive from primitive anxieties associated to the attacks directed to the primitive parental figures.

When children of both genders turn away from the mother's frustrating breast they turn to the father's penis, seen simultaneously as an object of desire and as a rival. Provided that early anxieties of damage towards the mother's body do not become excessive, the solution of the oedipal configuration should take place: "in the little boy the identification with the penis will lay the basis for heterosexuality, whilst turning to the father's penis as an object of desire will contribute to homosexual trends" (Etchegoyen, 2002, p. 26).

The first bodily experiences, the internal world experiences, that organise the ideas of masculinity and femininity, also start at birth, long before the child is mature enough to acknowledge the difference between genders, as Freud had argued. The developmental studies emphasise the importance of the unconscious communication between the parents and the child. The unconscious processes of the parents, as well as the way they conceive/organise themselves into "male" and "female", and their interrelation, become striking elements in the unconscious fantasised elaborations of the child, having consequences in his/her future physical, affective, and cognitive development. In the context of psychoanalytic thought, a rich and complex conception of internal world has emerged, well differentiated from the initial one, classically based on the physicist perspective—which insists on conceptualising the "masculine" and "feminine" around the conscious perception of the biological differences between genders. Verhaeghe, in his text "Phallacies of binary reasoning: drive beyond gender" (2004), sets out, in an enlightening way, the phallacy of binary reasoning, which arises from a biologisation of the mental apparatus, particularly visible in traditional approaches to sexuality and gender.

Initially, the concept of psychosexual identity was considered independent from the biological body. However, the traditional and rigid binary view of the two sexes and the two genders, seems to have settled into the theoretical formulations. The themes regarding masculinity and femininity are no exception: we tend to repeat approaches, generalising in an excessive manner, regardless of whether we are dealing with different objects and realities.

Given the specificity of the psychic reality, one's representations about gender and sex arise from the drives and the objects inherent to them (Verhaeghe, 2004) (where the psychic movements, created by Eros and Thanatos in their opposition, are related with the nuclear issue of the origins—specifically, the origin of sexually distinct life forms). Thus, the autonomy of the drive asserts itself as something much more relevant than the autonomy of gender which, in essence, is organised as a result or consequence of the drive's autonomy. Verhaeghe adds that the gender is only an expression of a wider problem: the drive, triggered by the experience of the original loss, tends to manifest itself repeatedly with the creation of genders and through the dynamic originated from its interrelations. Therefore, the gender differentiation is a secondary item that should not be interpreted in a binary way. On the contrary, masculine and feminine are always associated, as are Eros and Thanatos.

In this sense, masculinity and femininity influence the sense of belonging to a gender and the manifest sexual behaviour. However, this masculinity or femininity is not pre-existent, but rather built in a complex and dynamic movement of intrapsychic relations, between several aspects of the inner world, that are expressed in multiple ways. Masculinity and femininity are surely different expressions, but they are in relation and co-existent (Benjamin, 2004). It will be the contact with the father's presence in the mother's inner world (which remits him to the primal scene's fantasies) that introduces the psychic space between the mother and the child in an almost brutal way. This enables the child to start organising the development of the symbolic ability, of subjectivity and, in this way, to be able to deal with the demands of the external world, through a profound reorganisation of the feeling of omnipotence. The idea of the "father-in-the-mother's-head" becomes an essential element that can facilitate the contact with the "yet-to-be-known" father (Ogden, 1992), and later on with the external objects. This period of internal transition, between the presence of the preoedipal omnipotent mother and the "mother as the father's wife", is a dynamic system, capable of organising first sexuality and then sexual identity. Thus, we see that the fantasies which refer to the primal scene are essentially a range of thoughts and feelings in a constant flow and evolution.

The constitution of masculinity emerges from the introduction of a third element, the father, on the condition that he offers himself as an identification object. This introduction begins in the contact with the "father-in-the-mother's-head", even before she realises it, when she presents herself as "mother-as-the-father's-wife". This process, in the construction of masculinity, has been the subject of strong controversy regarding the identification movement towards the male universe and, simultaneously, an effort towards denial of the primary feminine identification. In the last two decades, Diamond has studied in depth the issue of masculinity and its development. Diamond (2004, 2004a, 2009) disagrees with the classical ideas of Greenson (1968) and Stoller (1968) regarding the boy's disidentification process from the mother as normal developmental experience. This seems to occur only inevitably when there exists a pathological dynamic, when the mother figure does not allow, or complicates, the entry of other characters in the child's mental life, thus adopting an intrusive nature, opposing the rupture of the primary attachment. The disidentification that Greenson proposes is, in fact, a narcissistic defence (Diamond, 2004, 2004a), which can, consequently, organise a severe superego, with a rigid sense of masculinity and impoverishment of the loving and affective relational experience.

The main criticism in Diamond's argument regarding disidentification, is that it is clearly based on a binary, simplistic, and reductive logic, where the masculine is defined by opposition to the feminine— "in other words, the most significant thing about being a man is not being a woman" (Diamond, 2009, p. 24). The author then proposes that the boy's separating movement is transient, but essential to help him differentiate and separate himself from the preoedipal mother— "However, this is not the same as 'disidentifying' from his internal maternal objects" (Diamond, 2009, p. 33).

Attachment studies have shown how the development of the masculine identity is facilitated by the good quality of the early mother-boy relationship (Fonagy & Target, 1996), and not by the quality of the separation. In normal development, a progressive differentiation should occur, different from the opposition feeling: a "watchful protective" father, typically in conjunction with a sufficiently "attuned" mother able to recognize her son's masculinity, helps to mitigate the severity of what might be potentially traumatising for the boy engaged in the separation-individuation process (Diamond, 1997, 2004, p. 53).

According to Diamond, for the boy it is no longer fundamental to waive the maternal identification to organise his masculinity. But it becomes essential to establish a solid affective relationship with both parents. In this way, the separation and individuation process can be experienced in a more fluid way, enabling the boy to condense the two references, in a process that seems endless throughout life. Introducing the relationship with the father results in the conceptualisation of the "genital mother" ("mother-as-the-father's-wife"), which is internally in conflict with the pre-genital mother. The unconscious identification with the father introduces access to sexual knowledge, leading to the discovery of the genital-mother. Blaming the father may be a way of trying to externalise the conflict. Nullifying the idealised stage of pre-genital ignorance, the unconscious contact with the father gives space to a different type of anxiety, which accompanies the reflection and awareness about the unavoidable incompleteness, and the confrontation with the threat of loss.

This experience leads the child to the loss of the feeling of omnipotence, as well as to the early loss of the symbiotic relationship with the mother. Intolerance of mental pain can lead the boy to the creation of a phallic self-image, in relation with the world, while seeking to control the object which is now separate from him. The opposing desires to discover the "new" world and maintain some of the primal qualities, "without obstacles, without roughness or differences, entirely smooth" (Chasseguet-Smirgel, 1986), can lead the individual to develop several internal solutions, with manifest qualities of a perverse mental functioning: using anal regression mechanisms, by which the differences are denied; idealising the regressive, pre-genital sexuality, thus installing a "blockage" on sexuality due to castration anxiety; and using a splitting of the ego and denial (Aragão Oliveira, 2008).

Moreover, when the father finds himself unable to mobilise the child's projections towards a possible genital object, the boy may assume a hysterical position when faced with the conflict, trying to return to the desexualised mother, assuming himself equally desexualised: "As Bollas observes, by idealizing her nonsexual characteristics, he turns her into a Madonna mother, and the self into a sexual innocent (i.e., 'a perfect little boy')" (Diamond, 2009, p. 35).

The relationship with the father should be able to facilitate the internalisation of the paternal imago, representing the genital masculinity, in which the adaptive phallic aspirations are merged with his relational connection abilities. In this way, the phallic characteristics become more "fit"; they organise themselves into integrated forms of the self that search for a complete and flexible relationship. The acknowledgement of one's incompleteness would be present, as well as the need for the object. The individual starts mobilising the phallic functions to support the contact with reality, understanding the other's differences, and developing a real empathic ability.

In psychoanalysis, the concept *phallus* usually refers to the symbolic aspects related to the notion of absence in the human condition, and to the experience of incompleteness: it is based in the distinction between to have or not to have (or the fear to stop having), to be or not to be (or the fear to stop being), of presence and absence, in a binary vision. However, I believe it is possible to make an internal reorganisation, which allows the individual to transform the *desire for* and the *desire to possess* into a precious mental instrument, serving Eros, and capable of promoting and creating (internal and external) connections. For this purpose, Birksted-Breen (1996) introduced the concept "penis-as-link" as an instrument of Eros. It is the mental function of "penis-as-link" which enables the connection of the parental figures, in the child's mind, marking the entrance into the oedipal structure: "it has to do with the tripartite world of the self in relation to the parents as different but linked to each other ... It involves the knowledge of difference and by the same token the recognition of incompleteness and need for the object" (p. 650). It is related to the use of real symbolisation, and its internalisation as a function: which allows enduring separation and the new connections, developing the symbolic capacity and the thought as a genuine instrument of internal change.

Its implications are essential in the mental functioning structure, now more complex: "good and bad, powerful and powerless, masculine and feminine are encompassed rather than being mutually exclusive. It refers to mental bisexuality" (Birksted-Breen, 1996, p. 652). Thus, the identification with the father's penis is not merely structured as an intrusive, penetrating element—the identification with the father's penis also has the ability to represent it as a connecting function between the parents (similar to Diamond's "genital-penis"), conceptualising the combined figure, for which, in my opinion, masculinity seems extremely necessary for the elaboration of psychic bisexuality. In the unconscious world, both *phallus* and *penis-as-link* can coexist, referring to specific symbolic functions. Also, the Kleinian breast and penis represent different functions to internalise: it is the breast that structures the functions *to be with, to be* and the *origin*; while the penis structures the functions *to do, to structure* and *to "move towards an end"* (Safra, 2009). Therefore, it is from the coexistence of both (in their own complexities) that it seems possible to develop a true mental flexibility, and a greater capacity to deal with the internal and external realities, in a more satisfying and rewarding way.

Masculinity and analytical relationship

The constitution of these primitive elements (the breast, the *phallus*, and the penis-as-link) seems to organise itself through unconscious fantasy, in a developmental stage previous to the onset of the perceptual and cognitive abilities (which enable children to differentiate these elements on the conscious level). The lack of real interaction with the father does not disable his presence and influence on a symbolic level. The link to the "Father", even to an absent one, is closely associated with the organisation of the ideal ego and to the development of superego structures, among other things. His presence can be felt by structuring different representations, which promote the development of primal mental states associated to the "self-observation" ability. In this way, André Green explains that under certain circumstances "it actually is impossible to speak of an early father murder because, considering the situation from the inside, the father is not yet a father, but rather just a 'would be' father" (Green, 2009, p. 37).

In the analytical context, by using the "presence through the absence" (of the therapist, which cannot be seen and is non-responsive), the analyst tries to refer the individual to very primitive elaborative processes, where the individual will become the latent organiser of different types of undifferentiated representations (words, affections, bodily states, actions, etc.). The theme of masculinity (placed essentially, in a floating way, between the phallic and genital representations), forces the analyst to internally contact his/her own psychic (bi)sexuality. It also forces the abnegation of the analyst/father, in order to phallically seize the genitality of the patient (Perelberg, 2009, p. 128). Thus, allowing the patient to conquer an inner space of a genuine elaboration, and development of the global use of his/her own relational and connection abilities, allowing the individual to love without controlling, or submitting to the other, and being able to recognise both the emotional dependency and the differentiated emotional needs of this other.

First clinical vignette

André was forty-one years old when he asked for analysis, feeling deeply lonely in a multiplicity of sporadic homosexual relations. During the analysis, he evokes, frequently, the following images: mist, casket, box, a thick wall surrounding him and preventing him from hearing and understanding. Later, they translate into a momentary drowsiness or, as he later started calling it, the "mind eraser", experienced in the relationship, and that erases things which are unconscious parts of him, not allowing them into the analysis (and into other areas of the mind). In the analytical relationship, this "mind eraser" is also felt as a countertransference effect, and the voice and attention of the analyst seem to drift into some kind of hypnotic sleep; transforming through transference, the "Father"/analyst in an absent and painful object. The work with the patient, usually stimulating and captivating, turns into something anxious for the analyst, invaded by feelings of helplessness and inability, and by repeated thoughts that the patient "is making me sleep", even in a rich sequence and important context.

During the first three years of analysis, the patient uses a notebook where he obsessively writes the unfolding of the sessions, a notebook that quickly grows into multiple volumes. However, it is only later that he finds the absence of the "analyst's voice" in the notebook, as he says in an admiring way, and afraid of my reaction: "It's like a description of the analysis, but the analyst is not there!"

He speaks of women and of the fear of intimacy. The patient had a girlfriend during his adolescence, with whom he had the rewarding experience of together discovering the sexed body—"but without intercourse!" He describes later harassments, by several women: "married, with children ... some more explicit than others. But I was always afraid; it was not physical repulsion, or anything like it, it was fear—of the devouring vagina!" Some sessions are filled with despair, where the patient cries because of the depressive void and the difficulty in finding the hope to change; the "maternal voice" seems to preclude the access to the "father figure". Of the analytic process he comments: "it is a kind of voice of the thought, of the spontaneity, the uncontrolled, that fascinates me, but I fear it for the madness it seems to bear".

During the third year of analysis, when he asks to increase the sessions to five per week, he realises that he has spontaneously stopped writing in his notebook, as if he felt he had some sort of internal notebook, built on the analysis, or the analyst, that exists within him: "it seems there is still a lack of syntax, grammatical flaws for some things, to translate some things into words". Then, he tells me about a dream, so distressing that it translates into enormous violence: he is going home (which belongs to his mother) in a bus (which is not usual). He passes through a military training camp. The bus is full, when he witnesses a horrifying scene: a group of three boys and three girls—"it is the same number of siblings I have!" he exclaims—are being pursued by special troops, who quickly kill the boys, and move violently on the girls. There is only indifference among the people in the bus, which makes him even more anxious and ready to panic. They first kill the two girls. One can escape for a few metres. She is particularly beautiful, fresh, and smells very good. But she is violently murdered. The bus arrives in his neighbourhood, he is completely panicked, and, at his door he sees an old colleague, who is also homosexual and whom he has not seen for many years. "I recently heard he has AIDS", he adds, which is actually one of his fears. He tells the friend what he has just witnessed, suggesting they hide inside the walls of the house. But, oddly, his friend does not react, and responds calmly, talking about going to saunas, meeting someone to have sex, etc. He wakes up very scared. André associated the protecting walls of the dream's house to the initial walls in the analysis, and to the function of erasing worries from the mind. The dream also shows the death of the male parts (the boys); it seems that these parts can only appear as a primary expression of the paternal figure (like the violent and brutal terrorist soldiers), who destroy the possibility of a relationship with the feminine (the girls).The scene of the full bus translates the experience of loneliness, unable to cope with anxieties, making a splitting of the ego (response from a homosexual friend), that perceives reality but denies the inherent emotions.

The minimisation of the father's role, or of the paternal function, which is organised by the creation of an illusion space, is the central element in the psychoanalytic understanding of the entire process. The patient's illusion of being the primary object of sexual interest of the mother figure, cancelling out the sexual and generational differences, refers to the existence of a mental functioning typical of the perversion (Chasseguet-Smirgel, 1978), where the discovery of the importance of the father's place in mother's mind will become essential. Coupling scenes with strangers, acted out more strongly during the first three years of analysis, were associated with the presence of the confusional and abandonment anxieties for which, however, the use of the penis (his own and of multiple partners) appears as a last defence, thus showing his independence, differentiation, and masculinity. In his own words, he relates in a fundamental and compulsive way with penises, which are necessarily attached to a person, "any person!"

At this time he dreams that he is coming to the session and finds the analyst, dressed in a classic suit and hat, and politely greets him and invites him to lie on the couch. However, the couch was the analyst's body—he associated the hat and the suit to the clothing of his deceased father, and to that which he sometimes wears to ceremonies (weddings, funerals, etc.). In the dream he lies down on the couch/analyst, where he sits comfortably, and with the analyst's arms around him. While lying down, he feels the analyst's penis getting hard, and that excites him at first, he feels surprised but calm, and wakes up. After a short silence he comments: "I feel that analyst's erection not as something sexual, but as if I was incorporating something from him—I do not know if this is the correct word?—it was as if I was able to bring some part of you".

Later, in his seventh year of analysis, when a greater tranquillity regarding his coupling experiences presents, André has a better understanding of his difficulties in tolerating differences, how he feels he is dying in the momentary separation from the other, and the terrible experience of fearing the end of everything: "I need this view of another about me, here in the analysis, I feel that view joining mine, to confirm that I am not a bluff, that I'm already a little man (smiles). But what would I like to be, for myself? … [silence] My older brother comes automatically into my mind … he is my father [his brother has the same profession as his father, in the same place]. But for that, to become someone, I still need an intermediary … to access to the Father …!" [Smiles, admired with his exclamation]. Meanwhile, he has made a significant professional investment, with academic and international recognition, and has started a emotional relationship with another man that has lasted until the present date, almost three years later.

In a more recent session, André mentions another dream, after describing a repeated discussion with his partner who accused him of being excessively worried about tidiness ("Just like my mother!"): "I am at home, sleeping, and my mother comes in screaming, 'What are you doing?' and I get stressed, as if caught doing something bad, like a small kid; as if I'm waiting for the outcome, and wake up anguished". He associated his mother's complaint to the fact that he took his partner to his home (that is why things are not in the place they should be). I interpreted that the mother appears with the "menacing paternal eye" that seems to refer to identity disorganisation, where things are not in place ("You bring men home and that is wrong"—his thought associated with the mother in the dream). The dream illustrates well the two periods of castration anxiety: the first by his mother, and the second, with the need for confirmation by the father, which has not appeared yet. The father's image seems to still be "swallowed" by the mother's phallus, which he looks for, in the analysis, as an organising element of the mental space and of the relationships. The prevalence of the primary identificatory model is present in this dream, where the patient, secretly identified with the mother, seeks to distance himself from the maternal, but not yet accepting the possibility of the other being and feeling differently (the depressive disappointment experienced repeatedly in the relationship with the partner).

Through the transforming movement promoted by the analysis, he realises that it is now possible to continue in that relationship: "In the past this would have been over, and I would be in the saunas and coupling rooms, jumping from penis to penis!" André's evolution seems to illustrate the differentiated use of the penis: as an object to conquer or as an object to relate to the other. The possibility of organising identifications with the idealised objects, allowing a complex set of fusional and differentiating movements, seems to only be possible in the context of a therapeutic relationship, where the analyst appears as composite figure, with merged maternal and paternal characteristics, allowing the ultimate development of a pre-genital sexuality. The difficulties in detailing the differences are confusing, where homosexuality tends to be organised primarily as a defence against the confusional anxiety between masculinity and femininity.

Second case

Mário sought help at a time of great inhibition and suffering, studying economics away from home, by choice, "to become big" and bigger than his father, a businessman with some success. However, he feels paralysed, in a permanent disparaging self-assessment and a state of deep depression. He has relational difficulties, and feels very lonely: "it seems I'm stuck inside myself; I lack the foundations of my house; the image I can express is of how children learn to ride a bike with some help, but when I look back to confirm the support, nobody is there". He only feels confident in his mother's house, in his home-town, that he visits weekly, where he can find an group of old friends, with whom he feels uninhibited and safe. He has had a girlfriend since he was fifteen years old, when his parents went through a dramatic separation. With this girl he has a relationship of strong emotional dependence, seeking her out, at times, during the week, just to feel her present and to calm down his anxiety. They have an unsatisfactory sexual life, with complaints about the inhibition of her desire. Mário complains that he feels he has a small penis (in both a metaphoric and a real sense).

In the analytic work for about seven years, Mário allows himself to get close to the father figure, manifesting, however, increasing hatred versus admiration for the father, experienced with great anguish and fear. The group of friends, that has been strictly identical since ado-lescence, is now allowing new openings and individualisations. He acknowledges the affective poverty in his relationships with women, despite feeling he has qualities for which he can be appreciated.

In the period when he starts living with his girlfriend, and when they begin their professional lives, the distance between them increases. At that time she has a health problem; she lives with enormous imbalance and violent regressive movements, moving back to her parents' house in another city, which leads to a progressive separation and break-up, that takes Mário back to his parent's divorce. His parents, even though divorced, maintain a somewhat dependent and paradoxical relational structure, where the strong father appears trapped by the uncontrolled, solitary mother. He complains frequently during the sessions: "I don't want to be like them". He fears loneliness and suffers tremendously. It will be, later on, the fatherly presence felt during the analysis that will allow him to integrate the hate and love impulses, where we find out that the intromission anxiety is much more intense than the fear of castration (Olmos de Paz, 2010). Both anxieties are associated with the fear of becoming symbolically castrated and submitting to the frag-ile introjected penis, in an endless cycle of dominant-submissive rela-tionships. The elaboration of the fantasy "my father wants me" (Denis, 1993), allowed him to emotionally invest in his individuation, with professional recognition, and to unexpectedly find a new love relation-ship, where sexuality is experienced in the complementarity of emo-tional closeness, that, at the age of twenty-nine, he discovers is possible and rewarding: "funny how my image of having a really small penis disappeared".

* * *

In the therapeutic relationship, the analysis should be conceived as the exercise of masculinity, in relation to femininity (intra and inter psychic), in a demanding movement regarding the analytic pair. Both can be seen as mental functions that relate in the analysis and in life (Vannucchi, 2009). In developing the mental space, the figure of the father and of the male appear as a midway point and balance between the child and the primary object, not allowing fusion and confusion and thus creating the possibility of contact with the world of differences. And, as Lima and colleagues stated, in an interesting debate on masculinity and femininity published by the Journal of Psychoanalysis (2009) of the Institute of Sao Paulo, "(I)t is not the matter of gender that is the most significant one, but the development of the ability to think (p. 34)".

References

Aragão Oliveira, R. (2008). O funcionamento perverso da mente. *Revista Brasileira de Psicanálise*, 42: 154–162.

Benjamin, J. (2004). Revising the riddle of sex: an intersubjective view of masculinity and femininity. In: I. Matthis (Ed.), *Dialogues on Sexuality, Gender, and Psychoanalysis* (pp. 145–171). London: Karnac.

Birksted-Breen, D. (1996). Phallus, penis and mental space. *International Journal of Psycho-analysis*, 77: 649–657.

Chasseguet-Smirgel, J. (1986). *Sexuality and Mind: the Role of the Father and the Mother in the Psyche*. London: Karnac.

Denis, P. (1993). Fantasmes originaires et fantasme de la pédophilie paternelle. *Revue Française de Psychanalyse*, 57: 607–612.

Diamond, M. J. (1997). Boys to men: The maturing of masculine gender identity through paternal watchful protectiveness. *Gender and Psychoanalysis*, 2: 443–468.

Diamond, M. J. (2004). Accessing the multitude within: a psychoanalytic perspective on the transformation of masculinity at midlife. *International Journal of Psychoanalysis*, 85: 45–64.

Diamond, M. J. (2004a). The shaping of masculinity: revisioning boys turning away from their mothers to construct male gender identity. *International Journal of Psychoanalysis*, 85: 359–380.

Diamond, M. J. (2009). Masculinity and its discontents: making room for the "mother" inside the male—an essential achievement for healthy male gender identity. In: B. Reis & Robert Grossmark (Eds.), *Heterosexual Masculinities: Contemporary Perspectives from Psychoanalytic Gender Theory*. New York: Routledge.

Etchegoyen, A. (2002). Psychoanalytical ideas about fathers. In: J. Trowell & A. Etchegoyen (Eds.), *The Importance of Fathers: A Psychoanalytical Re-evaluation* (pp. 20–41). East Sussex: Brunner-Routledge.

Ferenczi, S. (1924). *Thalassa: ensaio sobre a teoria psicanalitica da genitalidade*. Rio de Janeiro: Martins Fontes.

Fonagy, P. & Target, M. (1996). Playing with reality : I. Theory of mind and the normal development of psychic reality. *International Journal of Psychoanalysis*, 77: 217–233.

Freud, S. (1908). On the sexual theories of children. *S. E., 9*: 207–226. London: Hogarth.

Freud, S. (1908a). Analysis of a phobia in a five-year-old-boy. *S. E., 10*: 1–149. London: Hogarth.

Freud, S. (1913). Totem and taboo. *S. E., 13*: 1–162. London: Hogarth.

Freud, S. (1921). Group psychology and the analysis of the ego. *S. E., 18*: 67–143. London: Hogarth.

Freud, S. (1923). The Ego and the Id. *S. E., 19*: 1–66. London: Hogarth.

Green, A. (2009). The construction of the lost father. In: L. J. Kalinich & S. W. Taylor (Eds.), *The Dead father: A Psychoanalytic Inquiry* (pp. 23–46). New York: Routledge.

Greenson, R. (1968). Disidentifying from mother: its special importance for the boy. *International Journal of Psycho-analysis*, 49: 370–374.

Klein, M. (1928). Early Stages of the Oedipus Conflict. *International Journal of Psycho-Analysis*, 9: 167–180.

Lima, L., Gomes, M. C., Aleotti, R., Holovko, C. S., Malzyner, M., Rocha, E., Mrianda, M. & Carasso, S. (2009). Feminilidades/masculinidades: Releituras. *Jornal de Psicanálise*, 42: 31–49.

Ogden, T. (1992). *The Primitive Edge of Experience*. London: Karnac.

Olmos de Paz, T. (2010). Male sexuality and its vicissitudes. Lecture at the 23rd Conference of the European Psychoanalytical Federation, London, March 2010.

Perelberg, R. J. (2009). The dead father and the sacrifice of sexuality. In: L. J. Kalinich & S. W. Taylor (Eds.), *The Dead Father: A Psychoanalytic Inquiry* (pp. 121–131). New York: Routledge.

Safra, G. (2009). Os registros do masculine e feminine na constituição do self. *Jornal de Psicanálise*, 42: 77–89.

Stoller, R. (1968). *Sex and Gender, Vol. 1: The Development of Masculinity and Femininity*. London: Hogarth.

Verhaeghe, P. (2004). Phallacies of binary reasoning: drive beyond gender. In: I. Matthis (Ed.), *Dialogues on Sexuality, Gender, and Psychoanalysis* (pp. 53–66). London: Karnac.

CHAPTER NINE

Intersubjective context of gender and sexuality

Emilce Dio Bleichmar

In a review of the psychoanalytic literature of the last few decades regarding gender, we can find a lot of work concerning this issue. However, despite intellectual acceptance of contemporary views of female development, many authors have found it difficult to assimilate these ideas fully in the clinical situation (Benjamin, 2004; Elise, 1997, 1998; Fast, 1990; Fritsch et al., 2001; Kulish, 2000; Lasky, 2000; Mayer, 1995; Richards,1996; Torok, 1979; Tyson, 1982). Meissner (2005) states that our thinking about these matters has undergone significant change and that we may be drawing closer to a more comprehensive and meaningful understanding. However, despite intellectual acceptance of contemporary views of female development, many authors have found it difficult to assimilate these ideas fully in the clinical situation Fritsch et al., 2001; Lax, 1995).

I have been working on the relation between the Freudian concept of primary femininity and contemporary views of gender (Dio Bleichmar 1991, 1992, 1995, 1997, 2002, 2008), and in this endeavour have also encountered many difficulties in regard to the acceptance of this close relation. One of these is the question as to whether the term "primary femininity" refers to a construct of Self as a female and feminine or to a sense of Self specifically derived from the female body. Elise (1997) suggests that we should derive the term "sense of femaleness" from the female body and reserve the term primary femininity for feminine gender identifications and identity. However, she observes: "a primary sense of femaleness can never in reality be separated from social meanings of gender" (p. 514). By introducing the idea of "social meanings of gender" I believe I can identify one of the difficulties in psychoanalysis for fully understanding and clinically applying this construct, which is so contemporaneous and important for female subjectivity. I refer to the implicit theory of a large part of the psychoanalytic community, which thinks that to speak in terms of "social meanings of gender" is foreign to psychoanalytic theories of development and, of course, female development.

At this time, I consider that in order to clarify the relations between gender and female sexuality we should take into account contemporary psychoanalytic developments concerning the intersubjective structure of the self and sexuality in both Anglo-Saxon and French literature. This implies a major change in dichotomous thinking: sex and gender, femininity/masculinity, the rigid binary code of castration, the phallic logic of yes/no, have/have not, as described by Jean Laplanche in Gender, Sex and Sexuality (2007).

Gender, sex, and sexuality

This is the title of one of the latest papers by Laplanche (2007) that seems central to me in the work of establishing conceptual distinctions regarding this theme, both in psychological development and clinical work:

1. The precedence of gender over sex, which overturns the habits of thought that place the "biological" before the "social".
2. The precedence of assignment over symbolisation.
3. Primary identification, which, far from being a primary identification *with* (the adult) is a primary identification *by* (the adult).

Gender

For Laplanche (2007, p. 212), the social unmistakably precedes the biological: gender comes first, preceding sexuality. What does this mean? What led John Money to propose the term gender in 1955 to designate the process of assignment made by doctors, parents, the town hall, the church, a declaration with assignment of the given name, assignment of parentage, etc. "It's a boy! It's a girl!" This announcement in turn sets in motion a chain of dimorphous responses, beginning with the blue or pink colours in the crib and of the baby's clothing, the use of pronouns and the universe of diverse behaviour, transmitted from person to person and embracing all the people the subject encounters, day after day, from birth to death (Money & Ehrhardt, 1972). This conception of the role of others in the constitution of gender identity, highlighted by a neonatologist, was introduced into psychoanalysis by Stoller (1968). Laplanche, forty years later, also wanted to stress that this assignment does not occur point by point nor is limited to a single act, but is a complex set of acts that extends into the significant language and behaviour of the family environment. The primacy of the other, the adult, and language are elements in common in the conception of gender in both Money and Laplanche. The latter expresses it this way:

> We can speak of an ongoing assignment or of an actual prescription. Prescription in the sense in which we speak of so-called "prescriptive" messages: in the order, then, of the message, indeed of the bombardment of messages". (p. 213)
> And what I consider the most important consequence of this: "the precedence of assignment over symbolization". (p. 219)

A review of the literature shows that quite a number of authors understand that gender identity includes well differentiated representations of the mother's and of the father's body before the child comes to terms with the difference between sexes (Dio Bleichmar, 1991, 1997; Elise, 1997; Fast, 1979; Mayer, 1995; Person & Ovesey, 1983; Stoller, 1976; Tyson, 1982: 1994). These papers are joined by others based on direct observation of early development (Coates, 2006; de Marneffe, 1997; Roiphe & Galenson, 1995).

Subjectively, nothing allows us to state that biological sex is intimately perceived, apprehended, and experienced by the child in any fashion that is separate or independent of gender, so that doubts and discussions on whether primary femininity is a construct of self as a female and feminine, or a sense of self specifically derived from the girl's female body, seem to clear up. The little girl knows that her body is the same as her mother's and different from her father's; that is to say, she has representations of her female body, representations that have been formed through primary identification (Dio Bleichmar, 1997).

With fine irony, Laplanche proposes a solution to the riddle of primary identification with the father of personal prehistory, which is outstanding for its clarity and simplicity: instead of "identification with", "identification by" (p. 214). Thus, the girl not only identifies with the mother but is identified by the mother as a girl, hears herself referred to as "she", just as "she" is heard as referring to her mother, and will be identified and referred to as "she" by her father, which is different from the person referred to as "he". Money (1955) accentuates this two-way process by adding another key piece: that with the mutual recognition of sameness—mother and daughter—differentiation from those who are different simultaneously takes place: the girl is different from her father and the father identifies the girl as someone different from him.

The core of the idea of gender is that boys, as much as girls, recognise and identify with the father and mother, respectively, and are recognised and identified by the father and mother as a boy or girl who is the same as or different from themselves. This idea is based on the intersubjective structure which configures femininity and masculinity from birth to adulthood, since male and female traits are psychologically open and identity changes throughout life, as we have observed over the last century. The process of identification occurs very early, as Freud formulated it in his conception of primary identification, but it is a process initiated and maintained by adults before the human offspring in turn initiates the active process of identifying with the mother's femininity. And what is the mother's femininity? Her gender: her gestures, figure, and ways of relating. Therefore, it is important to emphasise not to try to separate representations of the body and identifications as different processes, since communication occurs within the attachment relation.

> For communication does not only pass through the language of the body; also the social code, and these messages are especially messages of gender assignments, all those provided by the adults close to the child: parents, grandparents, brothers and sisters. Their fantasies, their unconscious or preconscious expectations. This domain has ultimately been very poorly explored, the domain of the unconscious relation of parents to their children. (Laplanche, 2007, p. 215)

The intersubjective aspect—the social meanings of gender—is constant throughout development, since the mother's and father's conscious and unconscious representations of the female or male are included in their modalities of interaction and in the way the couple relates to each other. The nucleus depends on the child's incorporation of a relationship rather than a figure, so that when children identify with their mother, the nucleus of identity they internalise is their mother's relationship with their father (Diamond, 2004). Thus, the girl's identifications with her father or mother pertain not only to the Oedipus complex, that is to say, to the father as a sexual object and the mother as a rival, or to the parental couple as a sexual couple, but to their performance in general as a man and a woman, that is to say, gender, in a much broader and general sense of masculinity and femininity.

The many mothers of the feminine self and intra-systemic conflict

1. Hey, there's a guy here (Mafalda's little brother).
2. Good afternoon little girl, is your mother in? (Mafalda): That depends. Which one?
3. What do you mean "which one"? Just how many mommies have you got?
4. One that I adore with all my heart ... another that harasses me with her soup ... another that protects me, another that yells at me ... another that's happy at home ... another that's enslaved for life to the house ... another that ...
5. (Mother) Mafalda, who was that?
6. (Mafalda) A salesman that was sold on that thing about that you've only got one mother.

The Mafalda comic strip points up humorously one of the most universal paradoxes concerning the mother: the same person, and the multiple changes of meaning and value which take place in the course of the life of any human being, especially a woman's.

Different relationships with the same person and multiple identifications having different valences in the girl's and the woman's subjectivity—all representations of the mother that will have structured the woman's self when she begins an analysis, which will be displayed for us in the transference. When we speak of the mother's image, even in its Kleinian version of the good or bad breast, what mother are we talking about or rather, what aspects or qualities of the multiple relationships with the mother have been distilled as organisers of the self, and how can we distinguish and analyse them for their optimal transformation during treatment? How do we view aspects of the mother's gender in the configuration not only of the daughter's gender but also of her sexuality?

The mother as oedipal rival

A married and professionally successful woman, thirty-five years old, who had demanded analysis because of many and various hypochondriac problems, had until recently expressed little concern with having a baby. She always expressed severe criticism of colleagues who are inefficient in their work, except one woman who had no children. While she was at a party she had seen this woman and her husband deeply engrossed in one another. She thought that this woman was pregnant and felt envious, jealous, betrayed, and outraged but could not understand why. In the session she finally said that she was going to be the last one left and that for the first time she felt badly that she hadn't thought about maternity until that moment. If we view this fragment of analysis from a classic perspective, a thirty-five-year-old married woman with no thoughts about becoming a mother, envious, jealous, and feeling betrayed when she sees a couple very much in love, we would think in terms of unresolved oedipal conflicts. If we look at it from the point of view of a theory which contemplates inherent conflicts of femininity as a gender, difficulties in developing and maintaining a professional career with maternity, we would understand problems associated with intra-systemic conflicts of the ego ideal. This means that the conflict is with the mother as a model of woman rather than the mother as a rival in a triangular oedipal configuration. She had many memories of her as a woman who had no life other than her house and her daughter, her complaints and several somatic problems, and she wondered whether she too was locked into a "sickbed grip". The patient felt great relief when she could understand how and why she had been rejecting maternity and had been denying the experience of other women, as, for example, her own analyst.

If the figure of the mother as a sick mother is understood as a representation resulting from her destructive rivalry, this may lead women who do not wish to reproduce this model of the feminine gender to feel guilty about abandoning the mother, as the clinical material provided by this patient seems to express through her memories that she could not leave the house while her mother was there in bed. This overlap in the same unconscious representation—"you've only got one mother"—of different relations (infantile attachment, self-preservative dependence, affective and emotional bonds, rivalry and competence, and consequently, different internal objects or representations of the same person), generates undesirable effects when the time comes to differentiate herself from the models of femininity represented by this mother, since differentiation is considered separation and rupture.

The mother as a representation of restrictions on sexuality

The understanding of the mother as being admired, envied, and hated for being the father's sexual partner is only an infantile scenario which is often not supported when the adolescent or woman discovers how unreal or fragmentary this evaluation was, in view of the anxieties, difficulties, and restrictions of the sexual life of many married women, even in our generation. Reflections on the restrictive aspect of maternity for personal and sexual life were common in the memory of this same patient: "I always felt indebted to her when I went out and other times I felt how could she go out dancing or with friends, now that I'm sick and she should take care of me." It is understood that the patient might not fervently desire to be a mother and also express relief that the analyst had a life apart from her, unlike her mother, who had no life other than her daughter and her complaints.

Greek and Roman myths, and today's publicity and movies as modern factories of them, place women as the main symbol of sexual pleasure. Women are used as the most powerful symbol of masculine sexual stimulation, whereas the reality in female subjectivity is quite another matter. Nothing allows us to take for granted that the primal scene has remained unchanged in women's unconscious in adult life, when we listen in our clinical work to the complaints of so many women about the lack of pleasure or opportunities to have sexual experiences without side effects such as guilt, persecution, or physical problems; and the long, long periods without any sexual experience in their life. "I don't remember having seen my mother approach my father or any other man erotically". "She shared her suffering in bed with my father with me". "My father always had other women for love and sex, my mother was just that, the mother or housewife, but not a woman". These statements—with overtones closer or farther from reality—are an expression of the opposite representation of the mother as a target of oedipal hate and envy and much closer to representations of the mother as a sexually devalued woman, so common in female subjectivity and so paradoxically and confusedly represented by the religious figure of the virgin mother.

The mother as an attachment figure and vicissitudes of the differentiation-individuation process

Discrimination of the relationship with the mother from the mother as a gender model allows preservation of the internal maternal representations as a secure attachment tie, even though the model of femininity offered by the mother is not reproduced. A woman aged forty, who has decided not to have children, still begins a second analysis with a female analyst (the first had been a man), because she now has doubts about her conviction. Analysis reveals the threats to life implicit in maternity, since her mother suffered from an autoimmune disease.

She has a very significant dream about a painting of a Madonna and Child in a very sweet and beatific scene, which turns into another in which the Virgin appears dressed in rags, with an expression of intense suffering, while the painter observes the scene and the child is behind him. Her associations lead the patient to think that her father never protected her mother and to connect with intense hate towards him and also towards her mother, since she adds that she cannot stand "suffering women".

The choice of a female analyst by a woman with serious conflicts with maternity is frequently understood as displaying "maternal transference with heavy preoedipal colouring". However, we could broaden our understanding to other meanings—if we take into account her comment about "suffering women" and the presence in the dream of a painter—as seen in so many paintings of the Madonna and Child—apparently detached from the suffering. Reducing our understanding to preoedipal terms may leave aside aspects of the multiform structure of the female self—wanting a child but not motherhood with its risks and privations—a self that has been configured not only on the basis of early identifications but on a dynamic, ongoing process of organisation throughout life. The suffering women taking charge of all the work and the responsibility of motherhood while a man/father is living his life, was a prevalent content of the subjectivity of the woman. Discrimination of the relationship with the mother from the mother as a gender model allows preservation of the internal maternal representations as a secure attachment tie, even though the model of femininity offered by the mother is not reproduced, as was the case of this patient who had actually had a close relationship with her mother, who had been able to provide her daughter with adequate care and a loving relationship. "The mother in rags" in the dream referred much more to the mother's shadows of pain, because of her frustrating marriage, than to sentiments of helplessness in the patient. The other bias in the lack of discrimination between conflicts in the relational world and intra-systemic conflicts in the female self structure would be to understand the problem in terms of an unfinished process of separation-individuation and therefore to propose oneself in the countertransference as a third, to separate the daughter from her mother and enable her access to desire—in this case, of a child.

As Lyons-Ruth (1991) differentiated so well in her revision of the stage proposed by Mahler, children do not need to separate in order to individuate, much less at twenty-four to thirty-six months of age, but to transform early attachment while preserving the relationship. In order to preserve this relationship, it is essential for women to differentiate their mother in her model of femininity—which they tend to reject because of the enormous changes which have produced a real expansion of horizons of the female ego ideal—from their mother as an attachment and caregiving figure, whom they can go on loving without losing this relationship.

A different modality, centred on the hypothesis of preoedipal regression, would consider her as having some extraordinary claim or possession of the mother due to a profound retreat from oedipal disappointment. What does oedipal disappointment mean? The implicit theory is that there is only one explanation: losing phallic desire and becoming a castrated woman. A different theory would lead us to consider that oedipal disappointment concerns the grip of the traditional model of femininity: a life devoted to others, and its consequences, somatic problems (Dio Bleichmar, 2008). The meaning of the internalised sick mother could represent the opposite of a woman envied for her sex life with the father and the product of her triumphant phallic strivings, with the stereotype of a depreciated person; something in connection with her self and the mother's self, with the female gender itself rather than her relationship with men: father or husband.

The dilemma today: expansion of models of femininity or phallic triumph?

We often find interpretations of clinical material of female patients in which phallic symbols appear as an indication of their use of the phallus as a compensatory illusion supporting their triumph over mother/ analyst, dodging the experience of envy, loss, and mourning. We will examine the dream of a very prestigious professional woman, married and with children, uncommonly beautiful.

> "She was instructing a woman, a beautiful assistant and colleague to her husband, how to cook, and organised knives of different sizes, asking her for the longest and largest one, which she couldn't find; the woman went out to get it but the stores were closing".

A classical interpretation would be that she emerges as the superior cook compared to her husband's beautiful assistant: she is "in the know" about everything—an indication of her use of the phallus as a compensatory illusion. Once again, her differentiation from the representation of a devalued gender—it is possible to be beautiful and not stupid, a professional woman and at the same time a very good cook, even better than her mother—is considered an attack on her mother and the analyst. Not a legitimate desire of her self but a phallic desire based on penis envy. Or, with a more benevolent clinical ear, a conglomeration image of herself as male and female. We agree with this idea, but in the sense of a good conglomeration image of herself with multiple aspects of the self: emotional, domestic, instrumental, and intellectual traits.

On the other hand, what would the interpretations be if we understood her anxiety about always being considered to be cutting off all the other women's heads, not because of her aggressiveness but because of her capacities and good qualities? The knives multiply wherever she goes, and her desires could offer the hope of finding a less competitive area. The implicit theory of some analysts is to view certain differences with respect to the stereotype of femininity as a woman's increased hold on her devitalised femininity, considering it a sad irony that in "having it all" she has nothing of real substance or satisfaction. This is to say that a contemporary conception of the expansion of feminine gender identity—that by integrating feminine and masculine aspects women may access more substance and satisfaction—continues to be understood in the terms of Riviere, who in 1929 considered that a professional woman who enjoyed herself sexually with her husband and was an excellent mother and housewife, concealed her phallic desires in a masquerade of femininity (Dio Bleichmar, 1997).

Conclusions

If we are to incorporate the concept of gender, we need to broaden our listening and become better attuned to the ways women are speaking about their restrictions of the self, the difficulties they face when they decide to differentiate themselves from their mother's model, and the importance of understanding and separating these anxieties from oedipal conflicts. This orientation could help analysis to free them from somatic and bodily preoccupations. I think that the implicit theory which makes it difficult to fully assimilate contemporary views on female development is based upon the idea that gender is a sociological issue and fails to recognise that it is a broad and complex structure of the self configured from the outset in the unconscious intersubjective exchange between parents and their sons and daughters. It is from this perspective that I consider that the concept of gender, which initially had only a sociological dimension—even though it was a physician who first thought about it—may be worked upon psychoanalytically, as a group of psychoanalysts have been doing.

Laplanche also remarks:

> Careful! We say "gender is social", "sex is biological". Be careful about the term "social", since it covers at least two realities that

intersect each another. On the one hand there is the general social or sociocultural. Of course it is in "the social" that assignment is inscribed, if only in the famous declaration from the outset , made on the level of the institutional structures of a given society. But what does the inscribing is not the society in general but the small group, those close to a person, the socii. That is to say, it is reality the father, the mother, a friend, a brother, a cousin, etc. It is thus the small group of socii that inscribes in the social, but it is not Society that does the assigning. (2007, p. 213)

In clinical psychoanalysis, generally speaking, the vast majority, indeed the totality, the "observations" posit from the outset, and without reflection, "the patient was a 30-year-old man" or "a 25-year-old woman", and so forth. Is gender supposed to be nonconflictual to the point of being an unthought issue from the beginning? (2007, p. 210).

References

Benjamin, J. (2004). Deconstructing femininity: Understanding "passivity" and the daughter position. *Annual of Psychoanalysis*, 32: 45–57.

Coates, S. (2006). Developmental research on childhood gender identity disorder. In: P. Fonagy, R. Krause & M. Leuzinger-Bohleber (Eds.), *Identity, Gender, and Sexuality, 150 Years after Freud*. London: IPA.

De Marneffe, D. (1997). Bodies and words: A study of young children's genital and gender knowledge. *Gender & Psychoanalysis*, 2: 3–33.

Diamond, M. (2004). The shaping of masculinity: Revisioning boys turning away from their mothers to construct male gender identity. *International Journal of Psychoanalysis*, 85: 359–380.

Dio Bleichmar, E. (1991). *El feminismo espontáneo de la histeria*. Madrid: Siglo XXI.

Dio Bleichmar, E. (1992). What is the role of gender in hysteria? *International Forum of Psychoanalysis*, 1: 155–162.

Dio Bleichmar, E. (1995). The secret in the constitution of female sexuality: The effects of the adult sexual look upon the subjectivity of the girl. *Journal of Clinical Psychoanalysis*, 4: 331–342.

Dio Bleichmar, E. (1997). *La sexualidad femenina. De la niña a la mujer*. Barcelona: Paidós.

Dio Bleichmar, E. (2002). Sexualidad y género. Nuevas perspectivas en el psicoanálisis contemporáneao. *Aperturas Psicoanalíticas*, 11 (www.aperturas.org).

Dio Bleichmar, E. (2008). Relational gender compensation of the imbalanced self. *Studies in Gender and Sexuality*, 9: 258–273.

Elise, D. (1997). Primary femininity, bisexuality and the feminine Ego Ideal: A re-examination of the female developmental theory. *Psychoanalytic Quarterly*, 66: 489–517.

Elise, D. (1998). Gender configurations: Relational patterns in heterosexual, lesbian and gay couples. *Psychoanalytic Review*, 85: 253–267.

Fast, I. (1979). Developments in gender identity: Gender differentiation in girls. *International Journal of Psychoanalysis*, 60: 443–453.

Fast, I. (1990). Aspects of early gender development: Toward a reformulation. *Psychoanalytic Psychology*, 78: 105–107.

Fritsch, E., Ellman, P., Basseches, H., Elmendorf, S., Goodman, N., Helm, F. & Rockwell, S. (2001). The riddle of femininity: The interplay of primary femininity and the castration complex in analytic listening. *International Journal of Psychoanalysis*, 82: 1171–1183.

Kulish, N. (2000). Primary femininity: Clinical advances and theoretical ambiguities. *Journal of the American Psychoanalytic Association*, 48: 1355–1379.

Laplanche, J. (2007). Gender, sex, and sexuality. *Studies on Gender and Sexuality*, 8: 201–219.

Lasky, R. (2000). Body ego and the pre-oedipal roots of feminine gender identity. *Journal of the American Psychoanalytic Association*, 48: 1381–1412.

Lax, R. F. (1995). Freud's views and changing perspectives on femaleness and femininity: What female analysands taught me. *Psychoanalytic Psychology*, 12: 393–406.

Lyons-Ruth, K. (1991). Rapprochement or aproachment: Mahler's theory reconsidered from the vantage point of recent research on early attachment relationship. *Psychoanalytic Psychology*, 8: 1–23.

Lyons-Ruth, K. (1999). The two-person unconscious: Intersubjective dialogues, enactive relational representation and the emergence of new forms of relational organization. *Psychoanalytic Inquiry*, 19: 576–617.

Mayer, E. L. (1995). The phallic castration complex and primary femininity: Paired developmental lines toward female gender identity. *Journal of the American Psychoanalytic Association*, 43: 17–38.

Meissner, W. W. (2005). Gender identity and the self: I. Gender formation in general and in masculinity. *Psychoanalytic Review*, 92: 1–27.

Money, J. (1955). Hermaphroditism, gender and precocity in hyperadrenocorticism: Psychology findings. *Bulletin of the Johns Hopkins Hospital*, 96: 253–264.

Money, J. & Ehrhardt, A. A. (1972). *Man and Woman, Boy and Girl: Differentiation and Dimorphism of Gender Identity from Conception to Maturity*. Baltimore, MD: Johns Hopkins University Press.

Person, E. S. & Ovesey, L. (1983). Psychoanalytic theories of gender identity. *Journal of the American Psychoanalytic Association*, 11: 203–226.

130 MASCULINITY AND FEMININITY TODAY

Richards, A. (1996). Primary femininity and female genital anxiety. *Journal of the American Psychoanalytic Association*, 44: 261–282.

Riviere, J. (1929). Womanliness as a masquerade. *International Journal of Psychoanalysis*, 10: 3030–3313.

Roiphe, H. & Galenson, E. (1981). *Infantile Origins of Sexual Identity*. Madison, CT: International University Press.

Stoller, R. (1968). *Sex and Gender, Vol. 1: The Development of Masculinity and Fmininity*. New York: Science House.

Stoller, R. (1976). Primary femininity. *Journal of the American Psychoanalytic Association*, 24: 59–78.

Torok, M. (1979). The significance of penis envy in women. In: J. Chasseguet-Smirgel (Ed.), *Female sexuality: New Psychoanalytic Views*. Ann Arbor, MI: University of Michigan Press.

Tyson, P. (1982). A developmental line of gender identity, gender role and choice of love object. *Journal of the American Psychoanalytic Association*, 30: 59–84.

Tyson, P. (1994). Bedrock and beyond: An examination of the clinical utility of contemporary theories of female psychology. *Journal of the American Psychoanalytic Association*, 42: 447–467.

CHAPTER TEN

Identity: a constellation of emotional experience and metaphors in childhood

Irene Oromí

Among the many cultural manifestations appearing in a Western world that is convulsed by a wide variety of factors of change, is the recently notable profusion of literature, films, and internet formats for children and adolescents showing young people with magical powers and male and female vampires. This, in the case of cinema, is expressed in fast-moving sweeps of scenes that imprint speed, submitting the viewer's mind to a powerful perceptual impact, along with resonances of sensations that are difficult to think about in isolation from the story being presented. One also observes bodily decoration with tattoos and piercing, sometimes in sensitive zones such as the tongue, penis, nipples, or clitoris. It seems to me that all this might have a meaning that goes beyond the purely ornamental aspect of fashion, and that it influences or feeds into the cultural packaging in which children's identities are developing in our times. The construction of personal, individual identity is woven over a background of bodily essence, including gender identity, and this entails a person effectively feeling what he or she claims to be.

I have been motivated to write this paper by one of my patients, whom I shall discuss in greater detail later. This was a small boy with difficulties of gender identity, whom I treated some time ago. I reflected on the clinical material, taking as my basis the vicissitudes of the object relations and the mesh of identifications in the bosom of the parental relationships. This drew my attention to a phase in the treatment which I called "refuge", in which the child expressed catastrophic anxieties when faced with the threat of separation from his mother, and one could observe sensorial enclaves that made his identity tremendously fragile.

From the perspective of my professional evolution, which has been moving in the direction of further, deeper study of autism in children (Tustin, Meltzer, Corominas, Ogden, Villoca) and its different psycho-pathological manifestations, I see more clearly the difficulties of my small patient in the primitive areas of his psychic organisation. In the course of the treatment I was able to observe sensorial enclaves and autistic nuclei, which is to say, problems in connecting the sensations of bodily experiences with emotions. This brought about alterations in the basic metaphorical processes required for coherence of thought and consistency and solidity of identity, all of which I shall discuss shortly.

In the early days of psychoanalysis Freud, who was then interested in biology and neurology, applied the microscope of his genius to the personality of his patients, developing psychoanalytic theory and a method that enabled him to probe ever deeper into the intimacy of the emotions, feelings, and fantasies that have been progressively under-stood on the basis of his proposals and further developed in the evo-lution of psychoanalysis. Hence, he referred to myths and proposed explanatory metaphors to explain the unconscious functioning of his patients. In his *Three Essays on the Theory of Sexuality* (1905), Freud expounds his ideas on child sexuality and the erogenous zones of the body, after which he continued developing his ideas until relating his contribution on the erogenous zones with stages of libidinal develop-ment, and proposing bodily metaphors to express this evolution in oral, anal, and phallic terms (1923). These contributions were subsequently expanded and clarified by Freud's followers.

In 1915, Freud identified instincts or drives, defining them as stim-uli "reaching the mind, as a measure of the demand made upon the mind for work in consequence of its connection with the body" (1915, p. 122). He introduces the concept of instinct in order to describe the work of making the connection between the body's needs and their subsequent mental expression. He suggests the need for linking "thing representation" and "word representation" as a basic element in thought processes, thus giving the body and its sensorial experiences an inescapable place in mental evolution. In his understanding of evolution of identity, Freud also presents an essential psychological reorganisation, that is, an elaboration of the Oedipus complex, entailing a structural concept, a universal and biologically determined organisation of desires, fantasies, and meanings. A positive Oedipus complex entails a genital level of sexual desires in relation with the progenitor of the opposite sex and implies heterosexual movements or impulses, while a negative Oedipus complex gives rise to homosexual love impulses towards the same sex.

In order to elaborate this central triangular conflict of impulses and oedipal fantasies, the child needs to be able to carry out complex mental processes, projections, and introjections, and must be able to think his or her emotions (Bion, 1963). Nowadays, new social forms have appeared in the Western world in which masculine and feminine are used as categories independently of sex. There is no clearly masculine or feminine reality and the form this takes very much depends on each society. Whatever the case, the child is born with the innate fear of being alone and the need to be cared for (Winnicott, 1972), and the infant's relations with adults promote the growth and development of his or her identity.

Usually, when a baby is born—or in ultrasound scans—the genitals can be observed, so that it is possible to say whether it is a boy or a girl. The post-foetal development begins along with the hormonal endowment that has already had its expression in the phase of embryonic development. The parents will feel that the newborn baby is their real child, the one they desired and who appeared in their fantasies, and the grandparents, relatives, and friends in each culture will influence the development of his or her genetic endowment. The child will learn to live, shaping his or her sense of identity, including gender identity, whether this is in keeping with the sex determined by genitals or not. For analysts working with children, the main issue is not what is masculine and what is feminine. The true analytical challenge is to understand each case individually, along with its motivations and its suffering.

Metaphor as a link between sensation and emotion

Returning to Freud's ideas on the "body-ego" (1923), one recalls that the newborn child satisfies hunger by sucking, while this satisfaction is simultaneously nourished by an agreeable sensation arising from the contact made by the mucous membranes of the mouth and tongue, which links up with the baby's autoerotism and the oral phase of sexual development. From birth, at the same time as the child is connecting to his or her body and the corporal sensations of the viscera (Lethonen, 2006; Lombardi, 2002), a link is also being established between mother and baby so that they engage in a sensorial-emotional exchange, thereby establishing the underpinnings of the latter's mental development. Before gender identity is constructed, it is necessary to form an awareness of oneself based on corporeal personal identity at the same time as fantasies in relation with the breast are being upgraded (Klein, 1930).

Authors such as Isaacs (1952) and Winnicott (1972) describe the unfolding of fantasies and experiences through body tissues. I believe this way of thinking is quite similar to Freud's when he says that in the beginning the ego is a "body-ego".

In their work with autistic children, Tustin (1990), Corominas (1991) and Viloca (2003) go deeper in their research and knowledge of bodily connections and sensoriality, suggesting that if the baby remains fixed on bodily sensations, and if these are not linked with the emotion arising from the presence of the parents, development of the metaphorical, symbolic process, along with that of thought, is obstructed and this affects the sense of identity.

If bodily sensations predominate and are not connected with emotion in the object relation, a situation of non-differentiation between mother and child is maintained. There is a deficiency of sensorial-emotional connections in the child and he or she fails to generate an image of himself or herself, and of the mother who offers protection against catastrophic anxiety. The development of the processes of metaphorical and symbolic thought is thus thwarted, exacerbating the feeling of a void in the face of this absence of emotional connection. Authors such as Bion, Meltzer and Odgen have studied and enhanced knowledge of these primary mental processes in what has come to be called "primitive psychism".

Psychoanalytic theory is woven through with metaphors, and metaphorical thinking has great interest for psychoanalysis because of the influence of primary bodily experiences in psychic functioning, and the links and interrelations established between neuronal connections and unconscious mental processes. For some psychoanalysts, symbolism appears through primitive connections. Melnick (2007), turning to the work of cognitive linguists, argues for the importance in psychoanalytic theory of bearing in mind unconscious conceptual metaphors characterised by connecting sensations and emotions such as soft-warmth with affection, and hard-coldness with the lack of this. These unconscious metaphorical primary processes establish links between bodily sensations and emotion and feeling (Modell, 2006). The metaphor transforms meaning between two dimensions of reality—sensorial and emotional—giving rise to awareness of emotion and feeling.

Underlying the difficulties of separation from the object are catastrophic anxieties, which have a direct effect on the construction of sexual identity. Sex, thought to be etymologically related to the Latin *secare* (to cut, divide), means separate-differentiate and, if sensations prevail, the processes of separation are not mobilised. Emotion is necessary for this, along with the metaphorical link that opens up the way for symbolisation.

Poor connection between sensation and emotion paves the way for the organisation of enclaves and false identity (Corominas et al., 2005; Winnicott, 1972), as happened with the case I shall present. In the analytical work, primitive sensorial experiences that have not found a way of connecting with emotion can be linked up in the relationship between patient and therapist. Micro-experiences and "micro-introjections", (Adroer, 1998) are very sensitive moments in the analysis in which a fundamental role is played by the patient's expression of metaphors at the point when emotional contact is made with the analyst, who recognises and contains them so as to be able to talk and think about them.

The connection between bodily sensations and the emotional contact with the analyst enables generation of "idiosyncratic metaphors" (Oromí, 2004), an expression of the intimacy of the primary bodily experience, and its expression as represented in a mental figure, expressed verbally or drawn and influenced by cultural expressions (Erikson, 1963), at the point of emotional connection with the analyst.

Understanding of metaphor is slow in children, but even when some are understood they are not accepted because they coincide with emotional physical contacts that evoke early and perhaps traumatic stages. These are not traumatic in the sense of physical aggression—the incubator, illnesses, war traumas, "embodied memories" (Leuzinger-Bohleber, 2008)—but because of the difficulties of making the connection owing to problems in the emotional experience in linking sensation and emotion and thereby establishing differentiation from the object.

Paying close attention to the metaphors presented by a child, whether spoken or expressed in drawings, at the time when the emotional connection with the analyst occurs, constitutes an "idiosyncratic metaphor", which permits the elaboration of personal experience, along with a proposal for a way out of the enclave along the path of feelings and symbolism.

Clinical material

The little boy whose case I shall present began his analysis at the age of six. His concerned, anxious parents asked for help after being advised to do so by the school because of his problems of concentration and learning. He also played with girls, was hit by the boys who called him a sissy, and dressed up as a girl at home. The father, in a harsh tone of voice, said that it was very difficult for him to bear what was happening with his son. The mother, who was very affected, was weeping and said she did not understand what had gone wrong and that she found the child very demanding. They both expressed their disagreements as to how to deal with this. The little boy spent a lot of time alone, playing with dolls and looking at fairytales.

The couple has a daughter already and they stressed in the anamnesis that they had again been expecting a girl, that with the six-month ultrasound they had been told the child was a girl, so it was a great surprise to learn at the birth that they had a son. They say that they do not understand what has happened because he was calm and "such a good, divine baby" until the age of ten months. He was breastfed for three months and then given a combination of breast and bottle until he was five months. The step to eating solid foods with a spoon was very difficult as the child showed problems in accepting differences.

The first time I saw the little boy, I was touched by his sad, fragile appearance. He was accompanied by his parents and, when he came into the waiting room, I told him that I had spoken with his parents and that now I was meeting him so we could continue together to try and understand what was happening with him. He comes into the consulting room.

Early manifestations

At the start of the treatment I was struck by his way of using his hands and the very precise content of his drawings. He drew, very fast and skillfully, fairies, dancers, and little doll-like figures with small balls instead of hands. I noted that he kept touching the radiator, exploring the heat, after which he touched the cold wall for contrast. The first month, he embarked on a sequence in which he came into the room, went over to the toy box, took out two sheets of paper, stuck them together, side by side, with sticky tape, and then drew a sun on one side and a moon on the other. Under the sun was a king and queen, a house and two trees and, under the moon, two trees, half a house, and a princess with no hands. I describe what I see in his drawings, telling him that he has joined day and night together. He listens and asks me if I could get him some white plasticine for the next session. As soon as he arrives, he starts using the plasticine to make some cubes on to which he wants to stick wild and farm animals in two groups, but he mixes them up. At the same time he says, "They hit me at school". He takes some paper, draws and cuts out a fairy with a magic wand, leaving its silhouette in the paper.

I remark that he is trying to separate the dangerous animals from the non-dangerous ones but he has mixed them all up and they cannot move either, because they are stuck to this soft white plasticine. I say that maybe he thinks or feels that he could be magic and make day and night come together, as he did in his drawing the other day (showing him the drawing I have described). He listens attentively and then does Drawing One. I tell him how he is showing me that he does things very well, that he is good at drawing but that, underneath it all, everything is totally confused, all mixed up. I am overwhelmed by a feeling of confusion.

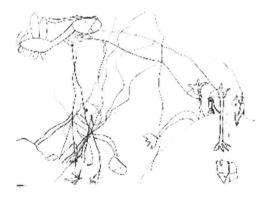

Drawing 1.

He leaves the drawing on the table, picks up two sheets of paper, sticks them together in the form of a bag and puts Drawing One inside, telling me, "For mummy". At the end of the session, he says that he does not want to leave and I remark that he is protecting himself at the moment of leaving and separation from me, that he is telling me that he does not know if things are going one way or the other, and that he is afraid of leaving his mummy especially if the children are hitting him at school.

Comments

When we first met, he connected with and explored the warm heater and the cold wall, investigating the relationship at a concrete level, testing the physical experience connected with the analyst, showing his skills of mastery over his hands, drawing figures, fairies, silhouettes in make-believe play as an expression of fantasies of sensoriality (Hernandez, 1992). The way he manages his hands fascinates me; his hands with the pencil, like a mouth with the nipple-penis (Corominas, 1979), take over my attention. I feel that he trusts in the relationship I am offering him and he is communicating his abilities in seeing the difference between representatives of day and night, but also how hard it is for him to keep them differentiated. It seems to me that, with this material, the child is revealing two levels of functioning, and one of them is connected with desires that the analyst, idealised as a fairy with a magic wand, will fix his problems, which is to say, separate his aggressive drives from his libidinal drives.

Nevertheless, he is unable to sustain the differentiation and expresses (Drawing One) a number of primary sensorial processes in which confusion appears (Tustin, 1990), expressed in a mélange of spatial and temporal relations and adhesive identification with white substances.

Sincerity

In the course of the following sessions, he tells me one day that he is going to make a story, asking me if I have brought glue. He sticks two sheets together, producing a bag, and is very quiet. I say that maybe he is noting that he has been left alone, remote from me, and that he is doing everything with glue. He says that it is for "My mummy". "What's the matter?" I ask. "Bedtime", he replies. I say that perhaps he realises that when he was a baby he was a very quiet baby who slept, adding that his parents had told me this when I met them before he and I started our work. He listens, carries on with what he is doing, says that he wants to cut the glue and then goes to the window, wanting to open it. I suggest that maybe we can talk and look at what he has noted when I was talking to him about when he was a baby.

He runs out of the room to the toilet. "I want water, water, water … I want it nice and cold".

I say that he can feel his mouth and wants nice, cold water to soothe the uneasiness that he is feeling. At the end of the session I feel uneasy.

The next time we meet, he rings insistently at the doorbell, comes upstairs to the consulting room and, on entering, wants to go straight to the toilet, shouting, "Poo!" He stays in the toilet for quite some time and I talk to him outside, asking if he is all right. He says that he is "not ready", and that "the poo's not coming out". I suggest that we go back to the room to see what happens. He comes out of the toilet and, on entering the room, goes to the playthings, picks up two small bits of wood, claps them hard together and then sticks them to the plasticine. I say that he has taken the hard wood and stuck it to something soft, that he is becoming aware of things when he comes here and when he is with me. I say that I understand that he is noting his mouth, which is thirsty, and also that he has got an anus that wants to do poo.

He says, "At school there's a little boy who's got problems", and "I want to do a story". He picks up several sheets of paper, sticks them together, draws princesses, saying that some of the girls call him "sweetie" and some of the boys want to marry him.

He rushes out of the room, shouting, "I want to do wee-wee". When he comes back he says that he is angry because the boys do not want to play with him and they call him "sissy". I listen, feeling daunted. He asks me for some squared paper and draws a princess and a little mouse with a very long tail.

I tell him that he feels that he is in a mess at school and that here, with me, he does not know what is happening, that he is noting feelings with his mouth, wants to do poo, and is not sure whether he is a girl or a boy, but he draws a princess and a mouse with a very long tail. He stretches, tearfully. As he is leaving he throws everything on to the floor and breaks the point on the pencil.

In the next session, he reclaims his piece of squared paper, drawing on it (Drawing Two) while also kicking under the table and emitting a high-pitched shriek, "Uuuuuuuu". I say that he is drawing four houses today, and he says "Yes". I then tell him that he can see there are connections underneath and that he is muddled up with all the strange things that he is observing in older people, but he is also aware of a mess down below, and he does not know if he is a boy or a girl.

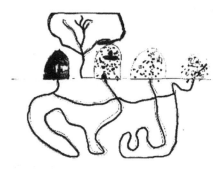

Drawing 2.

He looks at me and breathes. I look back at him and comment that he is noting air in his lungs and strange sensations down below, like before when he was moving his legs and going "Uuuuuuuu". I then ask, "What's going on down there, at the bottom of your tummy?"

He decides to colour one house red and another blue and marks them with dots. "I'm thirsty, I'm thirsty". I say that he is noticing his mouth again and the need for water, and to understand what he is noticing in his body and in his family. When it is time to finish, he finds it hard to leave.

Comments

The child is attempting, at a higher conscious level, to organise his thought and he draws four houses. He opens up about his problems at school. I think that he is connecting with his family and the underlying inter-linked relations. Yet, at a primary level, the troubled aspect appears and he seeks to connect with his erogenous zones in a more vital way and he recognises bodily sensations. Nevertheless, he feels stuck to his mummy and becomes agitated when it is suggested that we should talk, so he goes off looking for the cool sensation that will relieve the heat that he is noting as an expression of the analyst's understanding warmth. It seems to me that, at this primary level, there are sensorial enclaves at work, associating the sensation of hardness with the father and that of softness with the mother. He does not accept gender differentiation. The idealised princess woman has a mouse with a very long tail at her side but this is difficult for him and he cries, expressing the power of hardness by throwing everything on the floor and breaking the point of the pencil.

Primary bodily notion: idiosyncratic metaphor

In a subsequent session he draws a figure in a skirt and with glasses, occupying the whole sheet of paper. He says that it is a detective. I say that he wants to find out what is happening to him and about the emotions that he is feeling.

The next time he brings a doll with breasts. He dresses it in a skirt and says that it is a boy. I remark that he can turn women into men when he is playing but we have seen that this mess-up is painful for him, and that he is coming here to find out what's going on with him. He takes some pistachios from his pocket and says that he is thirsty. "I'm thirsty, mummy". I go with him to the bathroom and he drinks a lot of water, after which he returns to the room and starts making small figures with plasticine. I say that he can make whatever he wants with soft material, that he can eat the pistachios his mummy gives him, and also that he wants to investigate what is happening. He throws bits of wood at me. I tell him that now he has realised that I am proposing that he should understand, and something hard comes out of him, like anger. He does a drawing.

Drawing 3.

At the same time he yells, "Suckyhead!" I describe for him what has happened and we look at his drawing. I tell him that this body feels that there is a shark threatening it from below. He says, "Irene, my head doesn't go with my body".

As I go back over this material I think that the child is trying to organise his gender identity as he angrily comes out of the soft-sensation enclave and connects with the analyst, which enables him to convey a very personal idiosyncratic metaphor, expressed in his drawing and his shout ("Suckyhead"). Emotional, he opens up and expresses his experiences of inadequacy. As for his gender identity, it would appear that, on a superficial level, he is more feminine, connecting with skirt/high-heels cultural aspects. However, beneath this one can see a shark/penis threat. It seems to me that the underlying threat is his difficulty in managing and articulating primary physical sensations. He has remained stuck in sensorial enclaves. He explores hard-soft bodily physical sensations as the very primary conceptual expressions of hard-penis and soft-breast. A delicate head that cannot integrate all the perceptions appears in his metaphorical expression. I wonder whether the thorax-abdomen tube lacks space to accommodate the visceral organs, and about his feeling of fragility in his identity.

Vampire couple—mosaic of sensations

In the next session, he looks at the things in the toy box and decides to go to the toilet. "I have to do poo", he says. He stays for some time in the toilet and from outside I can hear him fiddling with the paper.

When he comes out I say that he has been playing with the paper and it looks as if he has done poo. He says that he has and, once back in the room, purposefully draws on a bit of toilet paper, a bed with two figures lying on it in what would seem to be a kind of coitus in which the upper figure is sucking and driving a stake into the one below. I comment that now I can see this couple, and he quickly replies, "Yes, vampires". I ask him why he has drawn this and he amuses himself by adding touches to his work. I suggest that we might think that these two together are not showing love, and that maybe he thinks that what joins them is fear of vampires. He listens. The drawing and the word "vampires" suggests to me an idiosyncratic metaphor that links up with his shouting "Suckyhead". This arises from the analytic relationship and is connected with a cultural fact. It is an image that he may have seen in a film and he expresses the experience of the union as oral and fusional vampire coitus. Male sexuality is presented as sadistic and bloodthirsty, which would be a reason for its being repressed.

After the separation of the holidays, during which the mother was unwell with back problems, I made an appointment for an interview with the parents. They had deep disagreements about the way their son should be treated. In one session he comes into the room rather edgily and rips up the paper on which he has drawn princes and princesses. I say that he is doing drawings in which he is marrying princes but perhaps he is worried about the fact that I can speak with his parents. After that he draws again.

Drawing 4.

This time, the child produces a compound figure, a mosaic of bodily perceptions and disconnected sensations. It shows confusion in differentiating penis and breast, and bodily fluids, milk, and tears. In this drawing he expresses a nucleus of muddled sensations, fruit of partial adhesive identifications, expressing the difficulties he has in the evolution towards his identity.

Final remarks

The child had primary difficulties in connecting bodily sensation with emotion and integrating bonding with the object. As defence mechanisms, he turned to confusion and an omnipotent use of his hands as products of his imagination, expressing fantasies of sensoriality in his drawings. I believe that my small patient managed his treatment with his hands, producing a lot of drawings, while also experiencing it intensely as he lived out the analytic relationship that made it possible to approach his catastrophic anxieties and to try to organise his identity. The woman, like the fairy with the wand of the early sessions, had to be ideal so that he could thus avoid all the conflicts involved in differentiation and identifying himself with the man.

The analytic relationship enabled him to establish an understanding emotional contact that brought him closer to his experiences of bodily recognition. The child produced an idiosyncratic metaphor (Drawing Three) in which he communicates the disconnection of a head that does not go with his body. He expresses a bodily interior with little capacity for viscera, lungs, or digestive apparatus, and a bagful of excitation at the lower part of his body. The head does not have the conventional sensorial organs but is a host of disintegrated explosive sensations. As his organisation progresses (Drawings One and Two) a fracture appears between the superficial level at which he attempts to resolve his difficulties by becoming a girl, and the deeper one.

Nonetheless, there are underlying reasons that work against his resolving his conflicts. From the multitude of connections that are produced in the primary experiences, he was incapable of producing the basic metaphors of primitive psychism by means of which he could keep weaving bridges between the bodily sensorial level and the emotional level in his bonding with the object.

The connection with conceptual metaphors makes it possible to observe an unconscious psychism in which the patient has trouble connecting warm-soft sensation with mummy-affection and the cold-hard ones with daddy-non-affection. The violence of the oral relationship—the vampire couple—leads me to wonder about a possible reason for his problems of integration. Union is sucking in a sadistic way, devouring, and the vampire relationship is not a creative one that might link up sensation with emotion and generate symbolism. The masculine has to be kept hidden because it is sadistic, and presenting oneself as a boy is sadistic, bloodthirsty. Perhaps the conflictual relationship between the parents, and the projection into the child of the mother's wishes for a girl, did not assist the emergence of an identity in keeping with his body; but, at a deep level, the problem was fixation in sensorial enclaves (Corominas, 1991) that are disconnected from emotion and that obstruct the generation of unconscious metaphorical thinking and symbolism, and this led to a fragile sense of identity. Seeking idealisation in fairies, princes, and princesses, he could not elaborate sensoriality and was incapable of renouncing the most archaic aspects of his being.

References

Adroer, S. (1998). Some considerations on the structure of the self and its pathology. *International Journal of Psychoanalysis*, 79: 681–696.
Bion, W. R. (1963). *Learning from Experience*. London: Heinemann.
Corominas, J. (1979). Oralisation et autres aspects de la fonction première de la main. *La Psychiatrie de l'Enfant*, 22: 2.
Corominas, J. (1991). *Psicopatologia i desenvolupament arcaics: assaig psicoanaltic*. Barcelona: Espaxs.
Corominas, J., Fieschi E., Grimalt, A., Guardia M, Oromí I., Palau M. & Viloca L. (2005). Comprendre el psiquisme primitiu, com ens ajuda? *Revista Catalana de Psicoanàlisi*, 22: 1–2.
Erikson, E. H. (1963). *Eight Ages of Man. Childhood and Society*. New York: Norton & Company, pp. 247–274.
Freud, S. (1905). *Three Essays on the Theory of Sexuality. S. E., 7*. London: Hogarth.
Freud, S. (1915). Instincts and their vicissitudes. *S. E., 14*. London: Hogarth.
Freud, S. (1923). The infantile genital organization, *S. E., 19*. London: Hogarth.
Hernandez, V. (1992). Concepte psicoanaltíc de la funció simbòlica: Simbolisme "sensorial" i simbolisme "metafòric". *Revista Catalana de Psicoanàlisi*, 9: 1–2.
Isaacs, S. (1952). Naturaleza y función de la fantasía. In: *Desarrollos en psicoanálisis*. Buenos Aires: Ediciones Horme, 1971.
Klein, M. (1930). Importancia de la formación del símbolos en el desarrollo del yo. *Obras completas de Melanie Klein, Vol. 2*. Barcelona: Paidos.
Lethonen, J. (2006). Nascent body ego. *International Journal of Psychoanalysis*, 81: 1335–1353.

Leuzinger-Bohleber, M. (2008). Biographical truths and their clinical consequences: Understanding "embodied memories" in a third psychoanalysis with a traumatized patient recovered from severe poliomyelitis. *International Journal of Psychoanalysis*, 89: 1165–1187.

Lombardi, R. (2002). Primitive mental states and the body. *International Journal of Psychoanalysis*, 83: 363.

Melnick, B. (2007). "No people are cold!": On young children's rejection of metaphorization. *Canadian Journal of Psychoanalysis*, 15: 1.

Meltzer, D. (1975). *Exploraciones del autismo*. Beunos Aires: Paidós, 1979.

Modell, A. H. (2006). *Imagination and the Meaningful Brain*. Cambridge, MA: Massachusetts Institute of Technology.

Ogden, T. H. (1989). *The Primitive Edge of Experience*. London: Jason Aronson.

Oromí, I. (2004). Algunes consideracions sobre el paper del jo en la contenció i elaboració de les ansietats catastròfiques: ús idiosincràtic de la metàfora. *Revista Catalana de Psicoanàlisi*, 21: 1–2.

Tustin, F. (1990). *The Protective Shell in Children and Adults*. London: Karnac.

Viloca, L. (2003). *El niño autista*. Barcelona: Ediciones CEAC.

Winnicott, D. (1972). Ego distortion in terms of true and false Self. In: *The Maturational Processes and the Facilitating Environment*. London: Hogarth.

CHAPTER ELEVEN

Furious with love—some reflections on the sexuality of a little girl*

Majlis Winberg Salomonsson

Our sexuality, love, libido, and our aggression, hate, destrudo, follow us like a red thread throughout our life. What is it that makes sexuality so interesting? It is not particularly effective, economic, or labour-saving. And yet, we devote ourselves to it to a great extent. Sexuality is always present in our minds. We seek it for pleasure, closeness, and confirmation. On a deeper level we may use it to heal a trauma, to charge inner objects with vitality, and strengthen self-affirmation.

What is sexuality then? Where does it emerge? Is it in coitus? Is it in adolescence, in adult life, or already in infancy? Freud suggests that · sexuality develops out of non-sexual needs from early on.

---

*This text is a slightly revised version of an article in *Kinderanalyse*, 2011 no 1: 21–35 (Wütend vor Liebe. Einige Überlegungen zur Sexualität einer Sechsjärigen) published with permission of the editor.

Infantile sexuality

Freud wrote:

> At a time at which the first beginnings of sexual satisfaction are
> still linked with the taking of nourishment, the sexual instinct
> has a sexual object outside the infant's own body in the shape of
> his mother's breast ... There are thus good reasons why a child's
> sucking at his mother's breast has become the prototype of every
> relation of love. The finding of an object is in fact a refinding of it.
> (1905, p. 222)

He continues:

> A child's intercourse with anyone responsible for his care affords
> him an unending source of sexual excitation and satisfaction from
> his erotogenic zones. This is especially so since the person in charge
> of him, who, after all, is as a rule his mother, herself regards him
> with feelings that are derived from her own sexual life: she strokes
> him, kisses him, rocks him, and quite early treats him as a substitute
> for a complete sexual object. (1905, p. 223)

An important moment is when the infant gets nourishment at the breast
and the lips; the tongue, indeed the whole mouth gets stimulated by
the breast and the warm milk. In this instance, nutrition and sensual
stimulation are inseparable. But in the moment when the functional
saturation and the non-functional erotic pleasure are separated—then
sexuality is created. The sexual object is separated from the functional
and can never again emerge in its original shape. Thus it is impossible
to find the first object. It is lost for ever.

The *Three Essays* and the description of the Oedipus complex play a
central role throughout Freud's thinking about sexuality. The Oedipus
complex is the cornerstone in his theory; it is a phase that everyone
has to go through in order to become human and leave the omnipotent
world of gods and goddesses.

Jean Laplanche's (1999a, 1999b) theories concerning sexuality imply
a return to the seduction theory in an ingenious way. His concept of *the
enigmatic message* implies that the mother conveys to her child her own
unconscious sexuality. This message remains enigmatic since the child

does not have the implements or language to translate it into something which has a meaning. This message will then be defined as something traumatic that cannot be symbolised; it remains a foreign body within the psyche and gives rise to constant new questions.

Sexuality becomes enigmatic to the infant. He gets the impression that the mother's sexuality is greater than himself. This can also give us, as adults, a feeling that our sexuality is greater than ourselves. Sexuality always includes a certain hunger, a curiosity and a desire to discover. Sexuality can thus be said to start with two things: a) the notion that something is greater than I am, and b) the discovery of longing that follows the object loss. Something is missing and thus the hallucination arises. Sexuality becomes the experience of desire trying to fill the gap. The other who is missing becomes enigmatic.

Let us look at sexuality in the clinical work and how it emerges in the analysis of a little girl.

Anna

Anna is almost six years old and has been in analysis for a year, attending four sessions a week. Her mother brings her to our sessions. When we meet Anna in the session she is carrying something in her hand and proudly shows it to me: "Look! An airplane!" She tells me that it can fly only sometimes, but only in hurricanes. Otherwise it will fall to the ground. She made it herself out of a few toothpicks marked with "Viking Line", some string, and a piece of a balloon.

Now the airplane is going to fly. I help Anna hang it up on a floor lamp. She hangs the string tied to the plane over a hook so the plane can fly up and down when she pulls or lets go of the string. She sits on the floor and flies the plane and is obviously enjoying it. She sings a song she has made up: "Where are you going, little girl? I am going to travel with my mummy and daddy". She shows me the plane and tells me that Viking Line is written on the wing. She says, "It is the first Viking wonder". We admire her creation together.

After a while Anna walks over to her cupboard and takes out a number of things: a babushka doll, a little muscle-man whom she calls Mighty Adolf (he is named after a character in the children's book *Pippi Longstocking*) with his car, and a train. Her play can start. The smallest babushka doll and Mighty Adolf are the main characters. She looks adoringly at him and his fantastic car and tells me that the little babushka is whispering, "Shouldn't we get married?" But he just drives around in his car and says to her, "Quiet now, I want to look at the airplane". Anna is flying the plane hanging on the lamp.

In a while, her play takes a new turn. Now Adolf does want to get married but she does not. Anna tells me that he is following her and appealing to her, "Beloved, dear woman!" Anna says, "But the girl is angry". Adolf pursues the girl and she runs away. She leaves on a train and he follows in his car. Anna is intensively involved in the play. Then the big babushka doll appears. Anna says, "Now her mother is coming" and adds that the mother is going to give birth to a baby. She says, "My dear little children". Mighty Adolf falls in love when he sees the little babushka. "But", says Anna, "her mother has told her about him and that frightens her". The little babushka runs away from Mighty Adolf, who tries in vain to catch up with her. Anna sighs and says, "And he was just in love". A truly sad story.

Phallicity

What does this clinical material reveal about the girl's sexuality? Anna wants to show me her airplane immediately, a plane that can fly only in hurricanes! It is the first Viking wonder and we admire it. We can regard the plane as a phallic symbol that she wants me to admire. I recognise this theme from the beginning of the analysis, when a main theme of Anna's play was dressing up in a costume with a long tail. I saw this as expressions of a wish, a fantasy, to have a penis. And she wants to show it off. In that transference I was the mother admiring her penis and she was the courting cavalier.

On her play stage we have two very different figures with entirely different roles:

He – drives his big car
    – plays with the airplane that he wants to watch

She – is angry
    – chases him away
    – admires him and whispers that she wants to be married
    – is afraid when her mother tells her about him

With whom does Anna identify? It seems to be partly with the mighty man who rushes after her and partly with the other character, the evasive babushka girl. A third identity, one with genital femininity, is glaringly absent.

These two identities are incompatible. Anna seems to be offended because she has only one gender, not both—and also because she cannot choose (Kubie, 1974). Children often build up a defence against this obstacle through denial. In child analysis we see boys openly expressing the notion of having both a penis and the ability to give birth, and we see girls' notions of being a girl and simultaneously believing they have a penis somewhere. Maybe it is inside themselves, too small to be visible—but it will grow!

In Anna's play the airplane will fly, up and down. We can look upon this play as a masturbation theme. The session begins with this manic and exciting play. Anna works with her fantasies about a penis; she seems to ask herself what it is all about. It is all very exciting. Anna seems to feel resigned and unable to deal with the fascination and fright about having a penis.

The primal scene

Anna thereafter creates a triangular situation: the little girl will fly away with her mother and her father. After this, the emphasis of the session is in getting married and having children, but there are always impediments.

The Vikings' first wonder conveys something about previous generations—Vikings who lived long ago, in prehistoric times, and this was their first wonder. Even the scene with the big babushka mother is a play about past history, generation upon generation. This brings us to the primal scene.

Freud categorises the primal scene, seduction, and castration all under the same heading: primal fantasies. He regards unconscious thoughts as having a sexual nature. The sexual function has a biological foundation, but the individual liberates himself/herself from it, and at an early stage sexuality takes the form of thoughts and fantasies. Freud's dualistic thinking permeates all his theories, including those on sexuality. This lends support to theorists who promote and emphasise the theory of biological determination. Others emphasise the Freudian notion that, from a psychological perspective, we are not born as man or woman; rather, our masculinity and femininity develop progressively. The biological part of the sexual drive is generally recognised and has been developed not least in the American tradition, while French psychoanalysis emphasises its symbolic function. The strength of Freud's own work lies precisely in his recognition of the complexity of the sexual drive and because he takes into account both these aspects.

Freud sees infantile sexuality as active from the moment of birth. The newborn baby's own body and mother's body are the first points of orientation in its environment, the starting point for its sexuality. This comes out in dreams and is acted out in different defence mechanisms and in symptoms. And in our material, sexuality appears in the form of symbolic play. Anna has many questions, and her play has several sexual themes. She seems to ask: Why should girls be afraid of boys? How are babies made? How did her mother have a baby? Anna seems not to have connected the function of the penis with the fact that the mother is about to give birth to a baby. Parental intercourse, the oedipal situation, is meaningful not only for the instinct for life but also as an organising factor for personality development. Anna avoids this scene and is therefore confused.

Session two

In our next session the mother arrives carrying Anna, who is fast asleep. I take the sleeping girl into my arms and carry her into the consulting room. I lay her on the sofa. I talk to her and try to wake her up. But she is asleep. She makes moves to swallow, which I have seen her do when she is tired and turns inward.

Anna is lying on the sofa and sleeps through the entire session, with her mouth half open and her arms stretched slightly outwards. I sit beside her and watch her. I think about how intense she is when she is awake: she loves me very much and hates me intensely. I am filled with warm feelings for her. I ask myself why she is sleeping now. I wonder if it is because of our session yesterday or if it is a reaction to the upcoming break. She provides no answers. She just continues to sleep.

When the session is over, I lift Anna up and carry her out to her waiting mother.

To sleep

The sessions with Anna are full of symbolism and can give rise to nearly mystical associations, not least in this session. Her sleeping makes me think of the young Sleeping Beauty, whose sleep prepares her for sexuality. From having actively worked in her play in our first session, Anna now falls into a deep sleep. Sleeping creates a distance to the sexual problems that figured in the play. When comparing Anna with Sleeping Beauty I ask myself what makes the fairytale sleep last a hundred years, until the time is ripe. As long as the girl's sexuality consists of infantile masturbation she is not mature enough for a sexual experience. The little girl is attached to the big babushka mother.

Anna's sleeping represents a powerful regression, in which she acts like a baby: she regresses from her oedipal conflicts. The big phallus becomes threatening and the encounter in the primal scene terrifying. To return to, and sometimes get attached to, the early mother represents a regression. Its function is to serve as a defence against this anxiety. In this way, Anna creates a breathing space from the painful confusion that characterises her inner self regarding questions of sexuality. Sleeping also creates a distance to me in the transference. It contains a striking mix of closeness and distance. When Anna slept on the sofa I clearly saw how she was far away from me, in her own world. At the same time she was very close to me, being simultaneously vulnerable and trusting. All these speculations are based on my countertransference since there was no verbal interchange during this session.

Session three

Anna is a little restless in the third session. She rushes into the room, chewing on a bun. She walks around the room a little aimlessly. She then walks over to her cupboard and takes out the things she used in the session the day before yesterday: Mighty Adolf and his car, the babushka doll, and the train. Anna comments, "Here comes Mighty Adolf, furious with love". He runs after the little doll and calls out, "My love!" Suddenly she says, "I have to take a wee now, wait for me". She gets up, pulls down her pants and scuffles towards the toilet with her pants around her ankles and says, "Excuse me for showing my bottom".

She soon returns to our room and continues to play. Mighty Adolf is running after his babushka and cries out, "Open, open!" She answers, "Never in my life. I'll never open for you". She puts the babushka on the train, and Mighty Adolf jumps into his car and follows the train. They drive around and around, the train up ahead and the car behind. Anna says, "He got tired of all this. Only small hearts came out into the air, not those tough snakes and such like. It was of course only for girls. He doesn't dare to tackle the train".

After a while Anna says that they are going to marry. They will have a church wedding. She places the doll on the car and Mighty Adolf at the steering-wheel. He drives them to the wedding. They should have presents with them, and the doll will receive a book. Anna scrapes a few flakes of paint off her paint-box to pretend they are small books. She hurts herself on a sharp edge and a spot of blood appears on her finger. She becomes visibly uneasy. I comment on her anxiety, but she continues to play without saying anything. Then the car turns over, the doll runs away—she does not want to get married: "Please dear God, make him detest me". Everything falls over and the books fly away. He calls out: "What did you do? You were going to get my nicest manly book".

Anna looks again at the cut on her finger and the spot of blood. She says, "There is, like, a lump there. Just think, if it's blood poisoning, do you have medicine for that?" I comment on her concern about her sore. She reaches towards my neckband, takes hold of my breast and says, "You have a lump there". I say, "Like you said about your finger". "Hmmm", she responds.

We are approaching the subject of boys and girls. She says that she knows how that is. "Boys have a willy. But by the way, I never think about that". There's a moment of silence. And then she continues, "Girls have bottoms, wee-bottoms". The session is almost finished and she is going to put her tights back on, but she puts them on backwards. Anna laughs. We talk about front and back. She says, "You know, the back, poo comes out the back, from the poo hole". I say that there are actually several holes. "Yeah, the front one is the wee hole," says Anna and then adds, "And there's another hole". She becomes agitated: "Yes, the one in between, where babies come out. I've discovered it. I didn't know about it when I was little".

The doorbell is ringing. Her mother is on the way in. Anna does not want to leave: "Just a little longer—she'll just have to wait". She wants me to give her a bun, she wants to go out to the kitchen, she wants to hide from her mother and pleads, "Tell her I'm not here". After a while she sighs and crawls out from her hiding place under the table and walks out to her mother.

Identifications

In this third session, Anna is again active. She is preoccupied with investigating questions about sexuality and thinks that our sessions are too short. The play sequences are condensed. Mighty Adolf and the babushka doll are about to be married but run into hindrances. In Anna's play he chases her in vain. They live in different worlds: she deals with issues of small hearts while he is occupied with tough snakes. The whole subject is connected with fear. Adolf's fear is evidenced by not daring to get up on the train—it was only for girls. She, on the other hand, does not want to get married and in the end she runs away.

Anna's identifications change quickly. One minute she is like Mighty Adolf—forceful and active, and in her fantasy she possesses the tooth-pick penis. The next minute deals with being castrated or deflowered, and the little babushka girl runs away in fear. Then Anna turns directly to me, in the midst of playing. She is preoccupied with the sore and the breast lump. She turns to me, the woman with the breast lump. She turns to me as a transference figure, but she also emphasises our similarity. We both have a kind of lump. In that sense I become an object of identification.

Several authors, for example Greenson (1968), claim that the mother is the first identification object and emphasise that while girls' development entails changing the love object, boys face the task of changing the identification object. Anna's material shows that girls' identification development is much more multi-faceted and complicated than it may seem at first sight. The early mother is only one of several mother figure identification objects. There is also the oedipal woman with a genital sexuality.

The hole

Anna has thoughts about the hole that she has discovered. It is the hole where babies emerge, and she remarks that she did not know about it when she was younger. Her discovery indicates that masturbation has entered her world now. Does this mean that she knows something about her female organs, even her inner organs? When we talk about boys and girls, she seems to have reached only a superficial level of rational knowledge but her play reveals an entirely different picture; she shows significantly greater depths of anxiety. Is this hole a shortcoming or an advantage? Is it a creative hole or a crater? The cavity seems so diffuse, and she finds it difficult to identify with her mother.

The main issue concerning sexuality in the analytic debate is female sexuality and the question of phallic monism. The controversy between

Freud (1918, 1925, 1931) and Jones (1938) was about this issue: Jones held that boys deny the existence of the vagina in order to avoid conflicts of envy, primarily regarding parents' intercourse, and the fear of castration. He wrote, "The idea of the vulva must precede the thought of castration. If there is no dangerous cavity to penetrate, there would be no fear of castration".

Chasseguet-Smirgel (1976) is another critic of Freud in this area, although she describes her objections in a different way. Her view is that the notion of sexual phallic monism has more to do with the fact that this theory tries to obliterate painful narcissistic insults, on two levels; in relation to a) the omnipotent early mother and b) the oedipal mother.

The desire to liberate oneself from the primitive mother leads children of both sexes to project control onto the father and his penis and to denigrate the specifically motherly organs and capacities. This is driven by the small child's feeling of helplessness. Here, Chasseguet-Smirgel refers to Freud's texts about the small child's experience of helplessness, "*hilflosigkeit*". She argues that if the little boy were entirely unaware of the female vagina, he would have no desire to penetrate her and thus have no need to envy his father in this respect. In this way the boy's narcissism would be partly protected.

Since the time of Freud, analysts have shown increasing interest in the very earliest development—the preoedipal period, with the early attachment to the mother. Our improved knowledge of the ties to the earliest object constitutes a breakthrough in the understanding of children's sexuality. We can see how it influences both the young girl and the young boy on a basic level. The mother is the first love object for both of them—and also their first hate object. We have learned a great deal about the ambivalent attachment of the girl to the mother, but today we also know more about both the young boy's fear and hate of this early mother figure.

Castration and penis envy

This brings us to the subjects of castration anxiety and penis envy. Both Anna's play material and her direct relationship to me suggest this theme. In the scene when Anna hurts her finger she is worried that it might be dangerous and cause blood poisoning. She also wonders if Majlis has a cure. Indeed, Anna has many questions.

Torok (1964) has studied questions about femininity and castration. She bases her ideas on the clinical observation that the analyses of women and also girls often contain periods of hopeless lamentation about the nature, imperfection, and limitation of their gender. It is as if the woman patient says, "My feeling of weakness, stupidity etc. is due to the fact that I am a woman—I have no penis". Torok's interpretation of this very familiar situation is this: what is actually lacking, hidden behind all these complaints, is the introjection of femininity. This is a problem in the relationship to the mother. The girl will experience her sexuality as if it were owned by the mother. This becomes a problem when the young girl grows up and wants to take command of her lust, sensuality, and dawning sexual feelings. In this situation she experiences that she is aggressively taking away something that her mother owns. The girl therefore makes the lack of a penis her own problem and she can thereby remain loyal to her mother (Yassa, 2002).

Anna says something while she is playing (the Babushka mother told the little babushka about Mighty Adolf and then she was frightened) that has associations to the Little Red Riding Hood (Grimm & Grimm, 1944) story. In the fairy tale the young girl is warned about the wolf. She is supposed to obey her mother; she may not leave the path but must go straight to her grandmother's house—that is, she should stay in the women's world and just be Little Red Riding Hood. Her mother warns her about the wolf's ravenous sexual appetite. In Anna's play the man is not the hairy wolf figure but Mighty Adolf's powerful apparition.

Furious with love

Mighty Adolf enters the stage, and he is "furious with love". He calls out "My love" and chases the little doll. Later, Anna turns to her analyst and says "Excuse me for exposing my bottom". Anna gives the picture of a little seductress. But we can see that the important thing is the excitement of this play. At the very moment that she is speaking about being furious with love, she has to leave to wee. The theme is exciting and frightening at the same time. Leaving the room to wee creates a release of tension, a relief, and a distance to me and the hot topic.

The play continues with Mighty Adolf driving around and the doll being perched on the car. The intercourse scene takes shape. Anna is trying to go beyond the infantile airplane masturbation, and she is struck with anxiety. She is worried about her bleeding sore. Everything gets out of hand and she is panic-stricken. Adolf is complaining, "What are you doing? You were to receive my finest manly book". Her perception of men seems to be that they deal with books, they are the thinkers. And how do people perform intercourse? Has it something to do with her getting a manly book?

The subject is associated with fright. Furious with love—an expression that reveals a link between fury, love, and fright. Anna presents a condensed picture of the essence of the dilemma of female sexuality. In Anna's words, how is it possible to be furious with love?

Fury – she has no penis, this wonder of the Vikings, something she perceives that the mother values highly
       – she does not have full access to the breast, that "lump" that can provide buns and nourishment

Love – of the mother, whom she in various ways wants to seduce, sometimes like a courting cavalier; she also approaches the mother with a more childish dependence
       – of the father, the man, this powerful, exciting figure with his penis

Fear – of her own sadism and attacks on the mother and her body
       – of the big penis and what it can do to the little girl
       – of the mother's revenge

Anna turns to me and grasps my breast. She uses the same words about my breast as about her own bleeding cut, the lump. Her finger is injured, and she fears for my breast and what she may have caused. Here the preoedipal roots of her problem surface. Her fury and hate have inflicted an injury on me, the transference mother figure. The punishment for oral sadism is that you must suffer, perhaps even get blood poisoning. The hate of the mother is a driving factor. In the tale of Sleeping Beauty, the evil fairy casts her curse that the girl must die. This can be reduced to a hundred years' sleep, but the evil can never be entirely vanquished. Why this hate of the mother?

Klein gives her opinion concerning this question when she speaks of the girl's fear of internal injury (1932, 1945). The cathexis moves from the frustrating breast to the penis, incorporated orally. Klein suggests that the envy is not only about the mother's capabilities but also the fact that she has the father's penis inside her. The girl therefore wants to sadistically attack the mother in order to take this organ from her. For Klein, female masochism is not sadism directed against herself but directed against the introjected object. Penis envy is not primary in the usual sense, but envy directed against the mother because she has the father's penis inside her body. Love is related to fury and is therefore frightening. The girl has the huge task of releasing herself from her dependence on, and identification with, the early mother. Only then can she meet the male, not in the sense of part-object penises, such as Anna's tough snakes in the air, but in the genital sense.

A common misunderstanding is that the penis is sufficient for this process to succeed. The tale of Sleeping Beauty illustrates the complexity of the situation:

> Then one day a prince was travelling through the land. An old man told him that there was a castle behind the thorn hedge, with a wonderfully beautiful princess asleep inside with all of her attendants. His grandfather had told him that many princes had tried to penetrate the hedge, but that they had become stuck in the thorns and been pricked to death. "I'm not afraid of that", said the prince. "I shall penetrate the hedge and free the beautiful Brier-Rose". He went on, but when he came to the thorn hedge, it turned into flowers. They separated, and he walked through, but after he passed, they turned back into thorns. (Grimm & Grimm, 1944)

Something powerful and potent is required of the girl to release herself from the infantile bonds to her mother and turn into a genital woman. This occurs through an identification with the genital mother, with her valuable, life-giving hole. In other words, she transforms the empty space into a life- and lust-giving space.

References

Chasseguet-Smirgel, J. (1976). Freud and female sexuality. *International Journal of Psycho-Analysis*, 57: 275–287.

Freud, S. (1905). *Three Essays on the Theory of Sexuality*, S. E., 7. London: Hogarth.

Freud, S. (1918). *Contributions to the Psychology of Love: The Taboo of Virginity*, S. E., 11. London: Hogarth.

Freud, S. (1925). *Some Psychical Consequences of the Anatomical Distinctions between the Sexes, S. E., 19*. London: Hogarth.

Freud, S. (1931). *Female Sexuality, S. E., 21*. London: Hogarth.

Greenson, R. (1968). Dis-identifying from mother: its special importance for the boy. *International Journal of Psycho-Analysis*, 49: 370–374.

Grimm, J. L. K. & Grimm, W. K. (1944). *The Complete Grimm's Fairy Tales*. New York: Pantheon Books.

Jones, E. (1938). *Papers on Psychoanalysis*. London: Ballière, Tindall & Cox.

Klein, M. (1932). The effects of the early anxiety-situations on the sexual development of the boy. In: *The Psycho-Analysis of Children*. London: Hogarth Press (1980).

Klein, M. (1945). The Oedipus complex in the light of early anxieties. In: *Love, Guilt and Reparation*. London: Hogarth Press (1975).

Kubie, L. S. (1974). The drive to become both sexes. *Psychoanalytic Quarterly*, 43: 349–426.

Laplanche, J. (1999a). *The Unconscious and the Id*. London: Rebus Press.

Laplanche, J. (1999b). *Essays on Otherness*. New York: Routledge.

Torok, M. (1964). The significance of penis envy in women. In: J. Chasseguet-Smirgel (Ed.), *Female Sexuality*. London: Virago (1981).

Yassa, M. (2002). Nicolas Abraham and Maria Torok—the inner crypt. *The Scandinavian Psychoanalytic Review*, 25: 82–91.

INDEX

absence, concrete presence of 56–58
"Achilles in Love" (Dunn) 17
adolescence 18, 52
    and notion of maturity 43–44
    case examples 36–39, 44–48,
        56–60
    discovery of sexuality and
        mentalisation of body 54–56
    Green Wheat (Colette) 40–42
    "hour of the stranger"
        (D. H. Lawrence) 35–36
    puberty/pubertal 35–36, 39–40,
        45, 54–55
    silence of 42–43
    transference/counter-transference
        37–38, 45–49, 57, 60
Adroer, S. 135
aggression 6–8
    and male impotence 71–72
Amati Mehler, J. 30, 71
analytical listening 91–92, 94, 97

androgyny *see* sexual
    undifferentiation
Aragão Oliveira, R. 106
Argentieri, S. 28, 73
attachment-individuation/
    differentiation 11, 124–126
autism 132, 134
Axelrod, S. D. 19

biological and cultural influences
    2, 4–5, 64, 73–74, 79, 103–104,
    118–120, 127–128
Bion, W. R. 7, 51–53, 88, 90–91, 133–134
biotechnology 65
Birksted-Breen, D. 107
bisexuality
    infant 51, 53–54
    see also psychical bisexuality
body
    discovery of sexuality and
        mentalisation of 54–56

161